THE GIFT OF TEARS

A 10-Week Devotional Journey

Annette Ford

WestBow
PRESS®
A DIVISION OF THOMAS NELSON
& ZONDERVAN

Copyright © 2023 Annette Ford.

All rights reserved. No part of this book may be used or reproduced by any means, graphic, electronic, or mechanical, including photocopying, recording, taping or by any information storage retrieval system without the written permission of the author except in the case of brief quotations embodied in critical articles and reviews.

WestBow Press books may be ordered through booksellers or by contacting:

WestBow Press
A Division of Thomas Nelson & Zondervan
1663 Liberty Drive
Bloomington, IN 47403
www.westbowpress.com
844-714-3454

Because of the dynamic nature of the Internet, any web addresses or links contained in this book may have changed since publication and may no longer be valid. The views expressed in this work are solely those of the author and do not necessarily reflect the views of the publisher, and the publisher hereby disclaims any responsibility for them.

Any people depicted in stock imagery provided by Getty Images are models, and such images are being used for illustrative purposes only. Certain stock imagery © Getty Images.

Unless otherwise indicated, scripture quotations are taken from the Holy Bible, New International Version®, NIV®. Copyright © 1973, 1978, 1984 by Biblica, Inc.™ Used by permission of Zondervan. All rights reserved worldwide.

Scripture quotations marked CSB have been taken from the Christian Standard Bible®, Copyright © 2017 by Holman Bible Publishers. Used by permission. Christian Standard Bible® and CSB® are federally registered trademarks of Holman Bible Publishers.

ISBN: 978-1-6642-9860-6 (sc)
ISBN: 978-1-6642-9861-3 (hc)
ISBN: 978-1-6642-9859-0 (e)

Library of Congress Control Number: 2023908098

Print information available on the last page.

WestBow Press rev. date: 06/02/2023

To my husband,

who loves me unconditionally,
supports me faithfully,
believes in me extravagantly,
and is my lover, mentor, and friend.

CONTENTS

Preface xiii
Acknowledgments xvii
Welcome! xix

Week 1: Tears of Praise

Praise: Day 1
Parable: Damaging Rains or Beautiful Flowers? 1
Praise: Day 2
Life Story: Becoming Jesus's Friend 4
Praise: Day 3
Insight: A Letter of Praise 7
Praise: Day 4
Life Story: Cemetery Praise 10
Praise: Day 5
Parable: Shining Stars 13
Praise: Day 6
Prayer and Reflection 16

Week 2: Tears of Confession

Confession: Day 1
Parable: The Garden Wall 21
Confession: Day 2
Life Story: Wonderfully Made 24
Confession: Day 3
Insight: Soft Sins 27
Confession: Day 4
Life Story: Meaningful Life 30
Confession: Day 5
Parable: Come to the Table 33
Confession: Day 6
Prayer and Reflection 36

Week 3: Tears of Identity

Identity: Day 1
Parable: Tin Soldiers and Sheep 41
Identity: Day 2
Insight: Dots and Stars 44
Identity: Day 3
Life Story: The Performer 47
Identity: Day 4
Insight: The Painting 50
Identity: Day 5
Parable: Belonging 53
Identity: Day 6
Prayer and Reflection 56

Week 4: Tears of Thanksgiving

Thanksgiving: Day 1
Parable: The Field of Corn 61
Thanksgiving: Day 2
Life Story: God Cares 64
Thanksgiving: Day 3
Parable: The Road of Renewal 67
Thanksgiving: Day 4
Life Story: I Will Trust You 70
Thanksgiving: Day 5
Parable: The Jewels 73
Thanksgiving: Day 6
Prayer and Reflection 76

Week 5: Tears of Joy

Joy: Day 1
Parable: Throne Room Joy 81
Joy: Day 2
Life Story: Joy in San Marino 84
Joy: Day 3
Insight: Count It Pure Joy 87

Joy: Day 4
Life Story: Where Is Joy?..90
Joy: Day 5
Parable: Heavy Burden..93
Joy: Day 6
Prayer and Reflection..96

Week 6: Tears of Healing

Healing: Day 1
Parable: The Good Shepherd and the Sheep.............................101
Healing: Day 2
Life Story: Wounded Healer..104
Healing: Day 3
Insight: Come to Me..107
Healing: Day 4
Life Story: Rooted in Heaven...110
Healing: Day 5
Parable: Flowers of Healing...113
Healing: Day 6
Prayer and Reflection..116

Week 7: Tears of Emotions

Emotions: Day 1
Parable: Out of the Mud and Mire..121
Emotions: Day 2
Life Story: We've Read the Last Page..124
Emotions: Day 3
Insight: Preparation for the Future...127
Emotions: Day 4
Life Story: The Gift at the Foot of the Cross..............................130
Emotions: Day 5
Parable: A Tree in the Path..133
Emotions: Day 6
Prayer and Reflection..136

Week 8: Tears of Purpose

Purpose: Day 1
Parable: Shadow Meets the Great Horse (Part 1) 141
Purpose: Day 2
Parable: Shadow Meets the Great Horse (Part 2) 144
Purpose: Day 3
Insight: What's the Point? 147
Purpose: Day 4
Life Story: The Front Lines 150
Purpose: Day 5
Insight: Don't Quit! 153
Purpose: Day 6
Prayer and Reflection 156

Week 9: Tears of Suffering

Suffering: Day 1
Parable: Shining Jewels 161
Suffering: Day 2
Insight: Suffering 164
Suffering: Day 3
Life Story: Far More, Far Better 167
Suffering: Day 4
Life Story: Joy Outweighs Pain 170
Suffering: Day 5
Insight: Reaping in Joy 173
Suffering: Day 6
Prayer and Reflection 176

Week 10: Tears of Encouragement

Encouragement: Day 1
Parable: A Lake of Roses 181
Encouragement: Day 2
Insight: Encouragement from God 184
Encouragement: Day 3
Life Story: Calgary Storm 187

Encouragement: Day 4
Insight: Consider Jesus 190
Encouragement: Day 5
Insight: The Blessing 193
Encouragement: Day 6
Prayer and Reflection 196

Farewell! 199
Notes 201

PREFACE

Tears. Tears of pain, frustration, or grief. Tears of anger, bitterness, or emptiness. When we think of tears, typically we consider the tears that stream from the depths of a storm-ravaged heart. But there are other tears as well. Tears of praise, confession, and identity. Tears of thanksgiving, joy, and healing. Tears of emotions and purpose. Tears of suffering and encouragement. These tears spring up softly, though often painfully, from a heart experiencing the gentle rain that brings daily growth.

Though we long for the constant sunshine of happiness and the comfort of a trouble-free life, we need the nourishing, refreshing teardrops of life lessons. Without tears, the garden of our heart becomes parched and desertlike, fruitless and barren. And so God offers us the gift of tears. If we accept this gift, we can look up through the rain and see the sunshine of God's love painting a rainbow of promise on the sky of our heart.

The gift of tears is a gift to our heart. Sometimes the tears spill over and run down our cheeks, but often they remain in the garden of our heart, where no one but God sees our pain or fully understands our joy. As we look with God's perspective at the gift of tearful times that He gives us, we see the beauty He is creating.

In this book, I share gifts that God has given me through my tears. You will read life stories of learning to trust God in deeper ways, especially in difficulties. You will experience parables from my times of quiet listening to God. And you will find insights I have gained from contemplating God's Word. This book was born from a sense that God said, "I have given you the gift of tears and the gift of turning tears into words." I am coming to understand that tears are a blessing, not a curse or a problem, and God invites us to thank Him for the tears in our hearts. May the words of this book, birthed from tears, refresh your heart and give you joy and strength in God.

To help you understand my life stories, let me introduce myself. When I was born, my Canadian and American parents, Murray and Florence Carter, were serving in church ministry in New Delhi, India. I entered a world where sacred cows meandered along streets crowded with brightly clothed pedestrians, honking cars, overcrowded buses, bicycle rickshaws, and dust everywhere. I was a little white girl in a world of brown people. Sometimes I wished I could be brown, too, because brown skin was beautiful. I treasured time with my parents and my sister Laura at home, at church, at Badkal Lake, and on picnics in the luscious gardens of Delhi. We spent our summer vacations in Mussoorie, a mountain village in the foothills of the Himalayas, where I enjoyed hiking, playing, watching wild monkeys scamper along the mountain paths, and eating peppermint sticks and fresh fruit from the man who carried it all in a hamper-like basket on his back.

We left India when I was ten and spent two years in Manitoba, on the Canadian prairies. I loved spending time on my grandpa's farm—collecting eggs and playing cards with Grandpa, making "dough boys" and drinking tea with Grandma, riding high on the hay wagon with my uncles, and trying to sit on my skinny uncle Roy and squish him for calling me, "Fatty, fatty two-by-four, can't get through the kitchen door." I spent many happy hours playing on abandoned farm equipment that spoke louder than a museum about the passing of time and progress of technology.

When I was twelve, we moved to northeastern Italy, a place of sunshine, seashore, and mountains, and of close friendships and deep loneliness. I saw history and art come alive, and I loved exploring the cobblestone streets and collecting shells at the Adriatic Sea. In my times of loneliness, I turned to God, listening to His words as I read my Bible, and writing letters to Him in my journal. He became my best friend.

I spent my high school years at the Black Forest Academy, a boarding school in southern Germany. My world expanded as I visited with German seniors at a nursing home, taught kindergarteners at a kids' club, helped as a teacher's aide at the elementary school, served on a worship committee at church, and participated in poetry club, soccer, drama, and choir. I enjoyed hiking with friends, making still-life creations out of tree bark, moss, and wildflowers when I was supposed to be running cross-country in PE, writing long letters home to my parents, and soaking in the beauty of the magnificent scenery.

After high school, I studied at Columbia International University (CIU) in South Carolina. I loved the emphasis on prayer at CIU, as well as walks with friends, fun at the beach, and the courses for my BA in elementary education and Bible and for my MA in intercultural studies and teaching

English as a foreign language. I met Stephen, my future husband, and grew to know him in Concerts of Prayer. After graduation, Stephen's dad helped me find a teaching placement in Toronto for the summer, and then I taught at a small elementary school in Chinatown. Stephen and I were married during spring break of my first year there. While I taught school, he served as the pastor of Toronto Alliance Church. I taught for two years, and then while I helped Stephen in the church ministry, our daughter Stephanie was born.

After four years in Toronto, we moved to Hungary. Our son Daniel was born there a year later, halfway through our language study. We worked in Hungary as International Workers with the Alliance Canada for eleven years alongside Hungarian Christians. I loved the deep friendships we formed there, the wildness of the Hungarian cowboy country, the majesty of Budapest, and the old Roman feel of our western Hungarian town. And I loved the poetry and beauty of the Hungarian language.

In response to God's call, we then moved to Almaty, Kazakhstan, where we worked with Tien Shan International School. Stephen also coordinated ministry among Christian workers in the country. We sensed God's call for us to have two more children, so Jonathan and Joanna were born while we lived in Kazakhstan. Almaty lies in the shadow of the snowcapped Tien Shan Mountains and is a blend of eastern nomadic, Turkic, and Russian cultures. While there, I worked at the school, cared for my preschoolers and teenagers, worked on an MA in Communication, and served as children's ministry coordinator at our church.

We returned to Canada for me to pursue a PhD in curriculum and teacher development from the Ontario Institute for Studies in Education (OISE), at the University of Toronto. After completing that degree, we spent an academic year teaching and serving at Ambrose University in Calgary. Then we moved back to Toronto, where Stephen is senior pastor and I am children and youth pastor at Toronto Community Alliance Church.

Toronto is now my home. After many moves and far too many goodbyes, I have come to love this city as my own. Toronto is a place of rest and beauty for me. From the downtown skyscrapers to the generous parklands, to the expansive waterfront on Lake Ontario, to the multicultural atmosphere, I am home. Not many people realize that a part of my heart is brown and sometimes I feel more at home with South Asians than with North Americans, that the Italian sea air blows through my veins, that the deep forests of Germany lurk in my heart and in my memories, that the Hungarian language echoes in my soul, and that I identify profoundly with ancient Kazakh nomads, as I, too, have lived a nomadic life. But along with all the others from many nations, I am home in Toronto.

And now I have recorded God's blessings to me through His gift of tears. I am proclaiming what I have seen and heard, so you will grow with me in knowing and loving God, and our joy will be complete.

> You yourself have recorded my wanderings. Put my tears in your bottle. Are they not in your book? (Psalm 56:8 CSB)

> We proclaim to you what we have seen and heard, so that you also may have fellowship with us. And our fellowship is with the Father and with his Son, Jesus Christ. We write this to make our joy complete. (1 John 1:3-4)

ACKNOWLEDGMENTS

My TCAC family. Thanks to all the children, teens, and adults at Toronto Community Alliance Church for your unwavering love for Jesus and for me.

My first readers. To all who read my manuscript in its various stages, thank you for your encouragement and comments that guided my writing and editing of this book. Special thanks to Daniel Ford, Laura Verderame, Carolyn Bruno, Sam Lee, and Jessica Lau.

My forever friends. Thank you to all my faithful friends who bless me on my journey. Whether we talk often or are just there, you enrich my life and give me hope and joy.

My faithful parents. Mom and Dad, thank you for your love, mentorship, and prayers for me all my life. You are my role models of Jesus's love and faithful service. Thank you for your stalwart support.

My loving kids. Stephanie and Dave, thank you for your advice about practical aspects of publishing and for your encouragement. Daniel, thank you for the months you spent trying out this devotional each day and for the helpful comments and suggestions you made. Jonathan and Joanna, thank you for standing with me throughout this process. I thank God for each of you and for your unwavering belief in what God can do through me.

My precious husband. Stephen, thank you for supporting me, believing in me, and loving me faithfully for over three decades of marriage. Without you, I would not be the woman I am today, and this book would not be written. Thank you for your unfailing love.

My wonderful Savior. Thank You, Jesus, most of all. You chose me, saved me, and invited me to be Your friend. Thank You for giving me life and hope each day. Thank You for blessing me with the gift of tears and the gift of turning tears into words.

WELCOME!

Come join me on a journey of parables, true stories, insights, and prayer activities. Five days of each week, you will find devotional thoughts, a personal challenge, Bible verses, and prayer activities. The sixth day will be for prayer and reflection. The book can be completed in ten weeks, but you can also travel this journey more slowly. Either way, take time to savor God's goodness.

The parables in this book are stories that emerged from my quiet listening times with God as He led me through journeys of healing and refreshing. I wrote them in a way that can include you, too, as you join me as one of "Jesus's friends." Each week, I also include life stories in chronological order. They describe my experiences of God's help, especially in my struggles. The insights are thoughts from my quiet times with God as I wrestled with questions and reflections from a biblical perspective. The prayer activities at the end of each day and each week lead you into various forms of prayer and allow for personal prayer, reflection, and application emerging from each parable, life story, or insight.

In week one, we journey through *tears of praise*. We experience parables of praising God even in times of attack and fierce storms. We look at my journey of becoming friends with God and praising Him in grief, and we learn the power of praise.

In week two, we bring our sins and weaknesses to God with *tears of confession*. We experience the joy of confession and forgiveness as we consider temptations of surrendering to darkness and fear, of questioning God's wisdom in the way He made us and the tasks He gives us, and of living in hypocrisy.

In week three, we more clearly see ourselves as God does even when we struggle with *tears of identity*. We see that although we might battle a sense of inadequacy or wonder about God's love for us, He invites us to find our identity in Him and in community with others who love Him.

In week four, we are refreshed by *tears of thanksgiving*. We see the blessings of choosing thankfulness in the seasons of life, in His faithfulness and joy in changes, and in times of renewal.

In week five, we experience *tears of joy* as God teaches us to choose joy in every circumstance. We see joy in His presence, joy in tough situations, and joy as we surrender our burdens to Him.

In week six, we journey through *tears of healing*. We see how God heals us to be a blessing to others and helps us find our roots in heaven. We consider what we can do with the wounds caused by others and how He transforms our brokenness into beauty.

In week seven, we find God's comfort in our *tears of emotions*. We see how God gives us His peace even when we feel stuck, helps us with our worries and fears, and clears unnecessary pressures from the garden of our heart.

In week eight, we explore *tears of purpose*. We discuss the purpose God gives us in experiencing his plans for us both individually and in community with others. We consider the times that we lack a sense of direction or meaning in our lives and how God fills us with His purpose.

In week nine, God ministers to us even in our *tears of suffering*. We see how He protects and frees us from attack, how He encourages us to keep seeking and following Him even when life is hard, and how He promises His blessings when we persevere.

In week ten, we conclude our journey together with *tears of encouragement*. We encourage others through roses of beauty, healing, and refreshing from God, and God encourages us as we turn our eyes toward Jesus and follow Him despite our excuses. We conclude by speaking blessings over others.

At the beginning of each week, we will create an Ebenezer stone to remind us of God's help. In 1 Samuel 7, when God's people faced attack and turned to Him for help, He defeated their enemies. Then the prophet Samuel set up a memorial stone, which he named "Ebenezer," or "Stone of Help," saying, "Thus far the Lord has helped us" (1 Samuel 7:12). In the next ten weeks, we will create our own Ebenezer stones as we journey together through *The Gift of Tears*.

Come with me now as we begin this journey together. I pray that on this journey your faith in God will be strengthened, your hope will be ignited, your joy will be rekindled, and you will overflow with love for God and others.

May the Lord make your love increase and overflow for each other and for everyone else, just as ours does for you. (1 Thessalonians 3:12)

The Lamb at the center of the throne will be their shepherd; he will lead them to springs of living water. And God will wipe away every tear from their eyes. (Revelation 7:17)

Week 1

Tears of Praise

I will exalt you, my God the King; I will praise your name for ever and ever. Every day I will praise you and extol your name for ever and ever. Great is the Lord and most worthy of praise; his greatness no one can fathom.
—Psalm 145:1-3

We begin our journey with praise. Praise is possible no matter what is happening in our lives. Whether we feel all is well, we have problems looming, we are dealing with issues we can't resolve, or we are losing hope, God invites us to praise Him. And we discover He works miracles as we praise His name.

I Praise You

God, You are my friend and companion. You take care of me even when no one is there. You are patient with me and love me just the way I am. When I sin against You, You keep loving me and waiting for me to return to You for forgiveness.
I praise You.
God, You are my protector and peace giver. You are my shield and defender. Darkness hides from You, and evil can never overcome You. I run to You whenever I am afraid. You are stronger than all evil, and when I say, "Jesus," all dark things flee.
I praise You.
God, You are my oasis in the desert. You bring refreshing streams to arid places and make them grow lush and beautiful. When I feel dry and empty, You fill me with Your newness and life. You are my hope and delight. Your presence is full of joy.
I praise You.
God, You are all-knowing. No problem is too complicated for You, and no one is hidden from You. You are wiser than the wisest person, because You are the source of all wisdom. When I ask You, You give me Your wisdom.
I praise You.
God, You are eternal. You have always been alive and will never die. You are everywhere. You are in front of me, behind me, and all around me. You are my provider. You give me everything I need.
I praise You.
God, You are my Savior who died on the cross for me. You are my Sanctifier who makes me holy and pure by Your Spirit. You are my Healer who can heal my body when I am sick and my heart when I am sad. You are my coming King who will one day take me to heaven, where I will be with You, surrounded by people I love and full of joy forever.
I praise You!

Ebenezer Stone: As we begin, choose a small, smooth stone and write the word *praise* on it. Place the stone where you will see it and remember to praise God.

PRAISE: DAY 1

Parable: Damaging Rains or Beautiful Flowers?

As Jesus and His friends walked along a beach, a terrible storm arose. Wind whipped the waves and fiercely drove the rain. Dark clouds billowed. The wind and waves were powerful and terrifying, full of constant motion, confusion, unrest, unpredictability, and change. Jesus's friends sensed a merciless lack of control.

Then Jesus opened their eyes to see the scene as He did. Instead of dark clouds, the sky was blue and sunny. Instead of biting rain, countless colorful little flowers swirled and danced in the wind. The flowers filled the air, rich in fragrance, full of joy and beauty. The wind blew constantly and powerfully, but the scene was not fear-filled because the lovely flowers soared, dipped, and twirled in the wind, supported and directed by the Spirit of God.

Jesus explained to His friends that some of them were feeling battered and tossed by storms of change and stress. They felt out of control and fearful of the uncertainties that clouded and battered their worlds. He invited them to see their lives through His lens. Instead of a fearful storm, they were experiencing a season of beauty and fragrance, with all events controlled and directed by His powerful Spirit. The billowing winds didn't carry dampening rains of fear and destruction but rather beautiful flowers of grace, joy, and peace in the sunshine of His love. He was in control of their world. They didn't need to be!

As Jesus and His friends continued to walk along the stormy beach, He urged them to submit their lives to Him even in their swirling, unsettling circumstances. He invited them to praise Him and continually ask Him to give them His eyes to see the beauty and fragrance He was creating.

Personal Reflection

Do you feel the wind and storms today around you or someone you love? If so, are you willing to ask Jesus to show you the beauty He is creating in the storm? He invites you to trust Him and not be afraid, because not only will He bring you through the storm but He will also bring good from it.

Write your thoughts here.

Bible Verses

> As they sailed, he fell asleep. A squall came down on the lake, so that the boat was being swamped, and they were in great danger.
> The disciples went and woke him, saying, "Master, Master, we're going to drown!"
> He got up and rebuked the wind and the raging waters; the storm subsided, and all was calm. "Where is your faith?" he asked his disciples.
> In fear and amazement they asked one another, "Who is this? He commands even the winds and the water, and they obey him." (Luke 8:23–25)

Prayer Activities

- When has God calmed a storm in your life (brought resolution to difficulties)?

- What storms are you or a loved one facing right now?

- Listen to "Oceans" by Hillsong UNITED, and in the space below, doodle what comes to mind as you listen. https://www.youtube.com/watch?v=dy9nwe9_xzw

- What do you sense God is saying to you in your storm?

- Write a prayer of praise to Him.

PRAISE: DAY 2

Life Story: Becoming Jesus's Friend

I FELT DEEPLY LONELY IN RAVENNA, ITALY, WHEN I WAS THIRTEEN. We lived in a house just outside of town, and I did school by distance learning from Canada. I had no friends nearby. With tears in my eyes, I wrote, "Friendship is very important. You cannot live without it. You don't realize it until you are isolated, friends miles and miles away. You need friendly companionship to survive in this lonely world. There is a special part of you saved solely for friendship. Without friends, it slowly, slowly dies, only to be revived someday by caring friends."

In those lonely months, Jesus reached out to me to be my deepest, most important friend. I had accepted His gift of salvation as a young child, so I knew He was my risen Savior, alive in heaven and present with me, but through my loneliness, He also became my best friend. If my life had been comfortable and satisfying, I might not have found the joy of being His friend and praising Him in every circumstance.

I started writing letters and poems to Jesus, expressing my heart to Him. One day I wrote, "Please, Lord, help me be like You. Help me smile and be pleasant even when tired. Help me not to worry but to give my burdens to You. Help me look to You when discouraged or upset. Help me trust in You, and give me Your peace." Another day, I wrote, "Lord, I have finally given my whole self over to You: my life, my health, my family, and their lives. My past, my present, my future all belong to You. Do with them as You see best to make my life victorious."

I continued in friendship with Jesus through my teen years, but while studying at Columbia International University, I began to wonder if my friendship with Him was worth the cost. I knew in my head that following Him was the best way, and I could give all the pat answers and corresponding Bible verses, but I had begun to understand more deeply that there was a cost in following Him. His path was not always the easiest or most comfortable. He was calling me to take up my cross and be willing to suffer or even die for Him. I wasn't sure I wanted that.

I struggled until I decided that friendship with Jesus, and the joy, fulfillment, and hope that comes from Him, were worth any cost. I wrote in my journal, "Go ahead, God. Make me like You. Yes, whatever it takes—sickness, death, sorrow, heartache, loneliness, grief—whatever, Lord. I pray that You will give me strength to keep fighting even when the hard times come. Take my fears, Lord." My heart filled with praise as I chose to follow in Jesus's footsteps, even if His path led to suffering or shame, because He was worth any cost. I would live for Him and praise Him no matter what happened.

Personal Reflection

Are you friends with Jesus? Have you committed yourself to follow Him no matter what the cost? Can you say to Him, "Whatever it takes, Lord, make me like You?" When we accept His gift of salvation, offer ourselves to Him, and choose to lift His name up no matter what the cost, we are offering Him a sacrifice of praise.

Write your thoughts here.

Bible Verses

> You are my friends if you do what I command. I no longer call you servants, because a servant does not know his master's business. Instead, I have called you friends, for everything that I learned from my Father I have made known to you. (John 15:14–15)

> Through Jesus, therefore, let us continually offer to God a sacrifice of praise—the fruit of lips that openly profess his name. (Hebrews 13:15)

Prayer Activities

- Take time to talk to Jesus now. Do you know Him as your friend today? If you don't, are you willing to accept His friendship through His sacrificial death for you? If you know Jesus as your friend, praise Him for the joy of friendship with Him. Write your thoughts to God here.

- Ask Jesus what He would like to say to you, and write what comes to mind.

PRAISE: DAY 3

Insight: A Letter of Praise

We can praise God in many ways. By speaking or singing words of praise, worshipping Him in our hearts, or writing our praise to Him, we lift up His name. One form of written praise is a praise letter.

My Precious, Holy Lord,

You raised me, a lifeless lump of clay, from the mucky, muddy mire. You began Your forming work in me and breathed Your powerful, refreshing, life-giving breath into my empty soul. You gave me a new name, a new hope, a new life. And You continually pour out Your grace, Your peace, Your joy, and Your love into my thirsty heart.

You use me to reveal Yourself to the world. You use my eyes to look with Your acceptance and not turn away in repulsion or indifference. You use my ears to hear the sighs of the hurting and listen to their aching hearts. You use my mouth to speak words of comfort and hope. You use my hands to touch others with Your tenderness and my arms to embrace them with Your healing love. You soften my heart when it is hardened and use it to pulse with Your grace toward even the most ungracious.

You delight me with Yourself, Your Word, and Your wondrous creation. You are my redeemer, my Father, and my friend. I love You!

With love,
Me

Personal Reflection

Do you realize the power of praise? Our words of praise bring great glory to God. He listens to our prayers of praise and pours out His goodness and peace on our hearts.

Write your thoughts here.

Bible Verses

> I will tell of the kindnesses of the Lord, the deeds for which he is to be praised, according to all the Lord has done for us—yes, the many good things he has done for Israel, according to his compassion and many kindnesses.
> He said, "Surely they are my people, children who will be true to me"; and so he became their Savior. In all their distress he too was distressed, and the angel of his presence saved them. In his love and mercy he redeemed them; he lifted them up and carried them all the days of old. (Isaiah 63:7–9)
> My heart is stirred by a noble theme as I recite my verses for the king; my tongue is the pen of a skillful writer. (Psalm 45:1)

Prayer Activities

- Write your own letter of blessing to God, praising Him for who He is and what He has done.

- What might God write to you in response? Ask Him for ideas and write them.

- Respond to Him. What would you like to say to Him now?

PRAISE: DAY 4

Life Story: Cemetery Praise

"Please, God, don't let Mommy and Daddy die!" As a young child, I knew if my parents died, not only would my heart break, but because I lived in India (and then in Italy and Germany as a teenager), I would have to return to Canada to stay with relatives whom I barely knew. So I made a bargain with God. If He kept my parents alive until I went to university, I would not complain or be angry with Him if He then made them die.

When the day came for me to head to university, I said goodbye to my parents and felt my inner world crumbling. I would never see them again. God had kept them alive as I had asked Him to, and now He would take them from me. Tears blurred my eyes as their car pulled away and drove out of sight. In desperation, I borrowed a bicycle and rode blindly out of town into the countryside.

I stopped at a cemetery, dropped my bike in the ditch, and walked into that lonely place. Throwing myself down on a grave, I wept. My parents would soon be lying motionless under a slab like this. How could I have imagined I would no longer need them when I reached the magical age of seventeen?

As I wept in the stillness of the cemetery, I poured out to God the pain of my breaking heart. Softly, almost imperceptibly, God poured back into me His incomprehensible peace. He loved me. His plan for me was good. Whether my parents died today or in eighty years, He would always be with me to comfort and help me.

A tiny seed of joy took root as my heart filled with praise to God, who was not out to get me but who tenderly cared for me. I did not need to fear. I was not alone. Joy and peace enveloped me and filled me with hope. My despair transformed into worship as I sat on the tombstone singing praises aloud to God. Even as I ached for my earthly father's and mother's arms, I felt the arms of my heavenly Father around me.

I left the cemetery that day with my heart full of praise. Bargain or not, God was good to me, and I felt His peace.

Personal Reflection

God cares for you in your times of joy and peace but also in your sadness and pain. When you pour out your heart to Him, He lifts you up and fills your heart with praise. Are you willing to exchange your sorrow for His joy? Take a few minutes to do so now.

Write your thoughts here.

Bible Verses

> I will exalt you, Lord, for you lifted me out of the depths and did not let my enemies gloat over me.
> Lord my God, I called to you for help, and you healed me. You, Lord, brought me up from the realm of the dead; you spared me from going down to the pit.
> Sing the praises of the Lord, you his faithful people; praise his holy name. For his anger lasts only a moment, but his favor lasts a lifetime; weeping may stay for the night, but rejoicing comes in the morning.
> When I felt secure, I said, "I will never be shaken." Lord, when you favored me, you made my royal mountain stand firm; but when you hid your face, I was dismayed. To you, Lord, I called; to the Lord I cried for mercy: "What is gained if I am silenced, if I go down to the pit? Will the dust praise you? Will it proclaim your faithfulness?
> Hear, Lord, and be merciful to me; Lord, be my help."
> You turned my wailing into dancing; you removed my sackcloth and clothed me with joy, that my heart may sing your praises and not be silent.
> Lord my God, I will praise you forever. (Psalm 30:1–12)

Prayer Activities

- Think of a time you felt discouraged or stressed. Did you turn to God in your stress? How was the situation resolved? If the situation is not yet resolved, are you willing to turn to God for help as the psalmist did in Psalm 30 (above)? Write the situation here.

- Write a prayer to God, praising Him for His help in your time of need.

- God is the one who lifts us out of our difficult situations and turns our sadness into joy. Pray Psalm 30 (above) out loud now as a prayer of praise to God.

PRAISE: DAY 5

Parable: Shining Stars

Jesus and His friends lay on their backs on the seashore at night, gazing at the millions of stars.

Jesus said, "Look at all the beautiful stars, there for your pleasure, there for you to delight in Me. Look for the little things around you. Look for the simple, everyday things that are beautiful, that I placed there to bring you joy in me. Let your souls rest in me and be at peace."

Then Jesus lifted them up and carried them among the stars, which were like jewels, beautiful, sparkling, and intricate. Jesus's friends saw that He shone brighter than any of the stars. They reached out and touched Him, and His light illuminated them so they, too, shone in the darkness.

Jesus introduced them to many others who shone for Him like stars. All the stars sang like an online choir, each in its own place, but all together, lifting up praise to God. Some stars joined a beautiful line of dancers, swaying and dancing in a long, wavy line. Others contentedly watched. All shone brightly together for Jesus in the dark sky, praising Him.

Then Jesus said to all His shining friends, "My children, come into My presence with thanksgiving and praise. Praise Me for who I am and thank Me for what I have accomplished. I am making you into people of praise.

"In praise, you will find strength and courage to persevere under pressure.

"In praise, you will till fields, plant seeds, and water them. And you will see Me bring the increase, the growth, and the harvest as you praise My name.

"In praise, you will fight battles and win victories.

"In praise, you will tear down strongholds and vanquish the enemy's power over those who are so far from Me. The battle is not yours. It is Mine. I am raising you up to be a light to the nations in your city and around the world."

Personal Reflection

Have you encountered Jesus in such a way that you are shining for Him? Do you praise Him, both alone and with others? Jesus invites us to come to Him to be filled with His light and shine for Him in the darkness through our praise.

Write your thoughts here.

Bible Verses

> You will shine among them like stars in the sky as you hold firmly to the word of life. (Philippians 2:15b, 16a)

> But you are a chosen people, a royal priesthood, a holy nation, God's special possession, that you may declare the praises of him who called you out of darkness into his wonderful light. (1 Peter 2:9)

Prayer Activities

- Pray this prayer of response to Jesus out loud.

  Jesus, I come into Your presence with thanksgiving and praise. I praise You for who You are and thank You for what You have accomplished. Thank You for making me into a person of praise.

  In praise, I will find strength and courage to persevere under pressure.

  In praise, I will till spiritual fields, plant seeds of truth, and water them. And I will see You bring the increase, the growth, and the harvest as I praise Your name.

  In praise, I will fight battles and win victories.

  In praise, I will tear down strongholds and vanquish the enemy's power over those who are so far from You.

  The battle is not mine. It is Yours. You are raising me up to be a light to the nations in my city and around the world.

- What else is on your heart to say to God now? Write it here.

- What do you sense He is saying to you?

PRAISE: DAY 6

Prayer and Reflection

PRAISE IS POWERFUL! IN PRAISING GOD, WE DECLARE WHO HE IS, fight His battles, and receive His joy.

In the psalm below, underline every word that describes God—who He is and what He does. I have underlined a few for you already.

> I will exalt you, my <u>God</u> the <u>King</u>; I will praise your name for ever and ever.
>
> Every day I will praise you and extol your name for ever and ever.
>
> <u>Great</u> is the <u>Lord</u> and <u>most worthy of praise</u>; his greatness no one can fathom.
>
> One generation commends your works to another; they tell of your mighty acts. They speak of the glorious splendor of your majesty—and I will meditate on your wonderful works.
>
> They tell of the power of your awesome works—and I will proclaim your great deeds. They celebrate your abundant goodness and joyfully sing of your righteousness.
>
> The Lord is gracious and compassionate, slow to anger and rich in love. The Lord is good to all; he has compassion on all he has made.
>
> All your works praise you, Lord; your faithful people extol you. They tell of the glory of your kingdom and speak of your might, so that all people may know of your mighty acts and the glorious splendor of your kingdom. Your kingdom is an everlasting kingdom, and your dominion endures through all generations.

The Lord is trustworthy in all he promises and faithful in all he does. The Lord upholds all who fall and lifts up all who are bowed down.

The eyes of all look to you, and you give them their food at the proper time. You open your hand and satisfy the desires of every living thing.

The Lord is righteous in all his ways and faithful in all he does. The Lord is near to all who call on him, to all who call on him in truth. He fulfills the desires of those who fear him; he hears their cry and saves them. The Lord watches over all who love him, but all the wicked he will destroy.

My mouth will speak in praise of the Lord. Let every creature praise his holy name for ever and ever. (Psalm 145:1–21)

Which characteristics of God in this Psalm resonate most with you today?

Using these characteristics, write a prayer of praise to God.

God, I praise You because You are ...

Look back over the past week on this devotional journey. Write at least one thing you would like to remember from the week.

WEEK 2

Tears of Confession

If we confess our sins, he is faithful and just and will forgive us our sins and purify us from all unrighteousness.
—1 John 1:9

As we think about our temptations and faults this week, let's remember that nothing we do or think can separate us from God's love. Like the father of the prodigal son in Luke 15, He is waiting with open arms to welcome us home. He longs to purify us and draw us into close friendship with Him.

Pride

Insecurity feeds it,
    Self-defensiveness protects it,
        Jealousy stems from it,
            Bitterness breeds on it.
Control shields it,
    Mercy flees from it,
        Anger grows from it,
            Despair rules it.
It breaks promises and lives,
    Friendships and homes,
        Churches and nations.
It makes man into his own god,
    People into objects,
        And God into a useful commodity.
It is impatient, unkind, and envious,
    Boastful and conceited,
        Rude, self-seeking, and easily angered.
It keeps detailed records of wrongs.
    It delights in evil and shuns the truth.
It never protects, never trusts, never hopes, never perseveres.
    It never allows for failure.
It fills its mouth with prophecies and tongues
    And its mind with knowledge.
It insists it knows fully and prophesies perfectly.
    It admits no imperfection or fault.
It talks like a child, thinks like a child, and reasons like a child.
    Even in adulthood, it does not forsake childish ways.
It convinces itself that the poor mirror reflection is reality,
    And seeing face-to-face is fearful and to be avoided.
        It wants to know fully now
            And seeks to never be fully known.
And now these three remain: doubt, despair, and pride.
    But the worst of these is pride.

Ebenezer Stone: Choose a small, smooth stone and write the word *confession* on it. Place the stone where you will see it and remember to confess your sins to God and live in purity.

CONFESSION: DAY 1

Parable: The Garden Wall

Jesus's friend walked in a garden with Him. To her left was a high wall that flanked the garden as far as she could see. They walked on a stony path by the wall. The garden to their right was beautiful, full of life and color.

On the other side of the high wall was darkness—colorless grayness and evil—the enemy's territory. She was tempted to go there—to be pulled through the wall.

A little robin flew to the top of the wall and landed there. A large, evil black bird immediately snatched it into the darkness. It seemed to be a sign to Jesus's friend that the enemy wanted to snatch her and take her into that dark place. She felt the darkness trying to pull her soul through the wall.

Jesus asked her to leave the wall and enter the garden with Him, but she didn't go immediately. She wanted to know what was in the garden, but she was also drawn to the forbidden wall. After deliberation, she left the dark wall and walked with Jesus down the path into the garden.

As they walked, she saw little, creepy bugs all over the ground—bugs of cynicism and negativity. She asked Jesus to take them away. He sent a great wind and water to wash through the garden. All the bugs were swept away to a place that Jesus sent them.

Then Jesus and His friend stopped at a beautiful fountain, and Jesus offered healing water. She accepted it and felt the healing begin.

She confessed sins of fear and commanded fear to leave in Jesus's name. She prayed for boldness and felt suddenly full of new courage.

She confessed despair and commanded it to leave in Jesus's name, and she saw a huge monster leave. She then prayed for hope and joy to fill her.

She confessed bitterness and commanded it to leave in Jesus's name, and sharp nails came out of her and left. She asked for peace and grace to fill her, and she felt flower petals and healing oil flow through her, making her grateful and beautiful.

She confessed rebellion and commanded it to leave in Jesus's name, and she asked for submission. As she bowed in submission to Jesus, a beautiful, sweet liquid flowed around her, like honey or sweet oil.

She confessed pride and worldly thoughts of prestige and success and asked for humility. Jesus filled her with a great, purifying light, and He healed her.

She turned and saw that the wall was gone. In its place was beauty and rest. Where the evil wall and its darkness had been, a beautiful meadow and mountain range filled the landscape. All around her was beauty and quiet.

Personal Reflection

What sins bring pain and darkness to your life today? What areas of darkness are you drawn toward? What is Jesus inviting you to get rid of in His name? For Jesus's friend, they were cynicism, negativity, fear, despair, bitterness, rebellion, and pride. What about you? Are you willing to confess your sins to Jesus today and receive His cleansing, beauty, and light instead of the darkness?

Write your thoughts here.

Bible Verses

> Have mercy on me, O God, according to your unfailing love; according to your great compassion blot out my transgressions.
>
> Wash away all my iniquity and cleanse me from my sin ...
>
> Create in me a pure heart, O God, and renew a steadfast spirit within me ...
>
> Restore to me the joy of your salvation and grant me a willing spirit, to sustain me. (Psalm 51:1, 2, 10, 12)

Prayer Activities

- If you are ready, ask Jesus to show you areas of your life that are pulling you away from Him and write them below. Confess them to Him and ask for His cleansing.

- Go for a walk in nature and find a flower, branch, rock, or something else that will remind you of the beauty God gives you in place of the ugliness of sin.

CONFESSION: DAY 2

Life Story: Wonderfully Made

I'VE BLOWN IT AGAIN. I'LL NEVER SUCCEED! GOD CAN'T USE SOMEONE WHO *fails like I do*. I remember the heaviness at the pit of my stomach as these words churned in my mind.

For many years, I felt too fat. In India, the ladies at church would pinch my round cheeks and compare me to my round father, saying, "Like father, like daughter." The boys on the street yelled, *"Moe-tee"* ("fatty") after me. When I was ten, I wore girls' size 14 husky jeans. In grade seven, I was the second heaviest in my class, and the top-scholar award didn't make me feel thinner! I was heavier than most of my friends in high school, so I lost twenty pounds, but in university, I gained it all back, plus some. I felt the agony of not losing weight and feeling I could never be acceptable to God or others unless I was thin. My parents always told me I wasn't too fat, but they were my parents, so they *had* to love me. Part of me was afraid to get married because my husband might reject me.

At university, I continued to feel like a failure. A serious dating relationship didn't last. I had no friends after the breakup because our relationship had been so exclusive. I failed a term of my practical ministry experience. I couldn't lose the weight I had gained. My grades were not as high as I expected because I didn't feel like putting in the effort. I didn't spend enough time alone with God, and I struggled with attitudes of irritability and pride instead of gentleness and humility. My kids' club at church was out of control. To top it off, I failed my driver's test twice.

My sense of failure persisted when I moved to Toronto after university. I didn't know how to dress right. I struggled to teach school with no set curriculum or textbooks. I felt overwhelmed in planning my wedding, and my mom was far away in Italy, so I left much of the planning to my mother-in-law. She willingly did it, but I felt like a dropout. I struggled to keep a clean house and perfectly fulfill all my roles as wife, homemaker, pastor's wife, schoolteacher, and then mother. I failed my driver's test twice more before I finally passed it on my fifth try!

In the midst of my feelings of failure and self-doubt, God blessed me through my husband.

"You're beautiful. Do you believe me?" he would ask.

"Not really," I would reply.

"I love you. Just the way you are."

He loved me deeply, unconditionally, whether I was thin or fat, talented or incapable, tidy or messy. He saw past my external beauty into my soul, and he breathed life, love, and freedom into me. He cheered me on. He encouraged me to soar like an eagle, follow my dreams, and become a woman of influence. He loved me as Jesus did. And I felt his love.

God was saying, "I want *you*, not what you can do. It's in your weakness that I can show my strength the most powerfully. I know you fail, but you're not a useless failure. I have chosen you and love you just the way you are. Please just give Me your whole self, failures and all, and I will use you in ways you can't even imagine."

Personal Reflection

Maybe you, like me, have felt inadequate and that God can't use you because you are a failure. The truth is that God loves you unconditionally and will use you as you are. When you feel inadequate and weak, turn to Him for strength instead of surrendering to discouragement.

Write your thoughts here.

Bible Verses

> Praise the Lord, my soul, and forget not all his benefits—who forgives all your sins and heals all your diseases, who redeems your life from the pit and crowns you with love and compassion, who satisfies your desires with good things so that your youth is renewed like the eagle's. (Psalm 103:2–5)

Prayer Activities

- Pray Psalm 103:2–5 (above) aloud to God.

- Circle one of these words: *forgiven, healed, redeemed, crowned, loved, satisfied,* or *renewed*. Write it on your mirror as a reminder.

- Write a prayer to God, praising Him for His forgiveness and love for you.

CONFESSION: DAY 3

Insight: Soft Sins

Some people struggle with tangible *hard sins*, like addiction to pornography, alcohol, video games, or food. Many others feel satisfied to have overcome or avoided those hard sins, not realizing they are ensnared by *soft sins*, which are easier to mask. Few people see them in us until they consume us, and even we can fail to recognize them in ourselves until they have hardened our souls.

James 3:17 says, "The wisdom that comes from heaven is first of all pure; then peace-loving, considerate, submissive, full of mercy and good fruit, impartial, and sincere." The opposite of these wise characteristics is "bitter envy and selfish ambition," which is "earthly, unspiritual, demonic" (James 3:14–15).

I struggled for a time with bitter envy. Although I recognized I was a reasonably effective communicator, I envied a colleague who was far more confident and creative in her communication. I felt angry that her ability surpassed mine. My selfish ambition said I should be at least as good if not better than she was. I needed humility that came from God's wisdom (James 3:13).

As we look at others who are more successful, more popular, and have larger influence and more followers, we can become envious. To get ahead, to build a better reputation, and to be more successful, we start to burn the candle at both ends. We get up earlier and stay up later to work harder, minister more fervently, and prepare more thoroughly. But the nature of candles is that fire consumes them. That fire in us, fueled by bitter envy and selfish ambition, leads to "disorder and every evil practice" (James 3:16). It begins to consume our relationships as we become impure, quarrelsome, inconsiderate, unsubmissive, lacking mercy and good fruit, showing partiality, and insincere. Ignoring the ashes of charred relationships with our colleagues, family members, and even God, we keep pursuing the dream of success with bold smiles on our faces and increasing emptiness in our souls.

Jesus demonstrated the opposite of bitter envy and selfish ambition. He knew the power He had in God, He knew where He had come from and where He was going, so he picked up a towel, knelt down, and served his disciples by washing their feet (John 13:3-5). His disciples had visions of being the greatest—ambitions to lord it over all, but Jesus served them so they could follow His example and develop to their greatest potential. And He invites us to do the same.

Personal Reflection

Do you struggle with envy toward others? Do you have selfish ambitions that are causing you to burn the candle at both ends? Are there relationships in your life that are suffering from your self-focus? Ask Jesus to show you what soft sins you are committing and may not recognize.

Write your thoughts here.

Bible Verses

> Who is wise and understanding among you? Let them show it by their good life, by deeds done in the humility that comes from wisdom.
> But if you harbor bitter envy and selfish ambition in your hearts, do not boast about it or deny the truth. Such "wisdom" does not come down from heaven but is earthly, unspiritual, demonic. For where you have envy and selfish ambition, there you find disorder and every evil practice.
> But the wisdom that comes from heaven is first of all pure; then peace-loving, considerate, submissive, full of mercy and good fruit, impartial and sincere. (James 3:13–17)

Prayer Activities

- What soft sins are pulling you away from God? Are you ready to confess your sinful attitudes like envy and selfish ambition and be cleansed by the power of God's Spirit? If so, humbly confess your sins to God now and commit yourself to Him.

    Heavenly Father, please forgive me for ...

- What can you do today to demonstrate the opposite of selfish ambition and bitter envy? How can you tangibly serve someone today, like when Jesus took on the role of a servant and washed His disciples' feet?

CONFESSION: DAY 4

Life Story: Meaningful Life

As a young mom and pastor's wife, I agreed with King Solomon as he wrote in Ecclesiastes that work by itself is meaningless. I informally surveyed people in our church, asking, "On an average morning, do you 1) wake up and wish you could sleep longer; 2) get up because there is work to be done; or 3) get up with joy and enthusiasm for the day ahead?" More than half of those surveyed wished they could sleep in longer, and I was one of them. Most of the rest admitted they got up just because there was work to be done.

When I was a child on holidays, I awoke with excitement for the day, but on schooldays, my mom woke me up whether I wanted to or not. In university, my alarm blared, and I dragged myself out of bed, looking forward to the holidays. When teaching school, I awoke with the fear of being late for work. As a new mom, I awoke because my baby daughter needed my care.

Some days, I struggled through life, seeing my work as a drudgery rather than a joy. I found that sometimes I did the *want tos* instead of the *should dos*, until the *should dos* became *have tos*. I said to myself, "I went to school and got good marks—for what? When I teach, the kids learn something. Then what? They'll never know everything. In my housework, I clean everything, and it just gets dirty again. Why do it? My life feels on hold for me with my baby. Will real ministry just take place in the future? Why bother working to overcome my failures? I'll just be disappointed."

As I spent time with God, He showed me that life is not a meaningless drudgery of work interspersed with all too short relaxation times. He told me, "The thief only comes to kill and destroy. I have come that you may have life, and have it to the full" (John 10:10).

I found that life became meaningful if I lived each moment of each day for God, seeking to do what He wanted me to do, the way He wanted me to do it. This meant not just having a quiet time with God in the morning, like a vitamin to last me all day, but spending time with Him throughout the day even as I accomplished my usual tasks.

Life took on a different outlook when I awoke in the morning and declared, "This is the day that the Lord has made. I will rejoice and be glad in it." It became a choice and then a way of life when I found meaning in the One who created me and loved me. He wanted to use me, even as a mom of preschoolers, for His glory.

Personal Reflection

Do you ever struggle in life, seeing your work as a drudgery rather than a joy? Do you complain to God and wallow in your inadequacies? God invites you to bring your burdens and complaints to Him and then leave them with Him. If you choose to confess your shortcomings to Him and give yourself to Him, He can use you right where you are, doing just what you are doing.

Write your thoughts here.

Bible Verses

> But thanks be to God! He gives us the victory through our Lord Jesus Christ. Therefore, my dear brothers, stand firm, let nothing move you, always give yourselves fully to the work of the Lord, because you know that your labor in the Lord is not in vain. (1 Corinthians 15:57–58)

Prayer Activities

- If you have been focusing more on your inadequacies than on God's power to overcome them, take time now to confess your negative thoughts about yourself to Him.

- What does He want to say to you now? Listen to His words of affirmation for you and write them here.

CONFESSION: DAY 5

Parable: Come to the Table

JESUS SAID, "COME TO THE TABLE!"

A long banquet table, covered with delicious-looking food, reached far into the distance. The plates were also filled with food, each beautiful in its presentation.

But no people sat at the table. And a terrible stench permeated the air. Then Jesus cut open some of the food and revealed complete rottenness within. All the food looked beautiful on the outside but was spoiled inside. The smell and rottenness repulsed anyone who might want to eat at the table.

The food there was the fruit of the lives of Christians who were not following Jesus wholeheartedly. Unlike the fruit of the Spirit that is pure and tasty, this fruit, though outwardly perfect and delicious looking, was rotting from sin and perversity. Under the attractive exterior lay sin that turned others away from Jesus. Places at the table were set for nonbelievers whom the church members invited to meet Jesus, but the nonbelievers were repulsed by the stench of the rotten food being offering them—by the sin-tainted testimony—so none of them would come near the table.

Then Jesus shook the table with great force. With a great swipe, He cleared the table of all the rotten food. The table became pure and white. Jesus then put simple, wholesome food on the table at each person's place—healthy fruits and vegetables. Soon, many people gathered at the table, eager to taste the wholesome goodness and receive new life. Then Jesus added great dishes of elaborate, life-giving food in the middle of the table. The food was enough for everyone and so much more beautiful than the original food had seemed, but this time it was pure and delightful. It smelled and tasted delicious. The people ate and felt deeply satisfied.

Personal Reflection

Jesus is calling us to confess our sins and let Him sweep our lives and churches clean. He longs for us to produce the wholesome, life-giving fruit of the Spirit, and He will use this fruit to attract others to Him. He will nourish us all with His amazing heavenly food, for His glory.

Write your thoughts here.

Bible Verses

> Put to death, therefore, whatever belongs to your earthly nature: sexual immorality, impurity, lust, evil desires and greed, which is idolatry. Because of these, the wrath of God is coming.
>
> You used to walk in these ways, in the life you once lived. But now you must also rid yourselves of all such things as these: anger, rage, malice, slander, and filthy language from your lips.
>
> Do not lie to each other, since you have taken off your old self with its practices and have put on the new self, which is being renewed in knowledge in the image of its Creator. (Colossians 3:5–10)
>
> But the fruit of the Spirit is love, joy, peace, patience, kindness, goodness, faithfulness, gentleness and self-control. (Galatians 5:22–23a)

Prayer Activities

- Draw a large banquet table below. On the table, draw different kinds of fruits.

- Label each fruit with the Fruits of the Spirit from Galatians 5:22–23 (above) and with other good characteristics that are opposite of sins that people in your church or community might struggle with.

- Ask God to cleanse your church from hypocrisy and from all sins and to fill your church with each of His good fruits.

- What do you sense God is saying to your church or community?

CONFESSION: DAY 6

Prayer and Reflection

G OD INVITES US TO CONFESS OUR SINS AND THE SINS OF OUR CITY.

Confess personal sins:

- Ask God to bring to mind personal sins that you need to confess. Write them in the space here.

- Confess the sins to God and ask Him to forgive you. To symbolize how He blots out your sins, cross them out as you confess them—even scribble all over them, so you can't read them.

- Draw a heart over each scribbled-out sin. Thank God for how much He loves you, and ask Him to fill you with His love.

Confess city sins:

- Now think of the sins of your city or town. Write them in the space here.

- As Daniel did in Daniel 9:4–20, confess the sins on behalf of your city.

- Scribble them out and draw a heart over each one, asking God to fill your city with His love.

Look back over the past week on this devotional journey. Write at least one thing you would like to remember from the week.

WEEK 3

Tears of Identity

The LORD your God is with you, the Mighty Warrior who saves. He will take great delight in you.
—Zephaniah 3:17a

And my God will meet all your needs according to the riches of his glory in Christ Jesus.
—Philippians 4:19

Perhaps you have wondered at times who you are and where you belong. This week, we will seek to see ourselves as God sees us, understanding that His love and acceptance of us are far greater than anything we can comprehend, and praying that He will continue to make us more like Him.

I Trust in You

My God, my Lord, my Master, King,
I give to You my offering:
My time, my friends, and all I am.
Use them, dear Lord, in Your good plan.

    I trust in You alone.
    You are the only one
    Who satisfies my soul,
    Who heals and makes me whole.
    Almighty God forever.

When I am troubled and distressed,
I trust in You for peace and rest.
I praise You, oh my Father-friend.
Your goodness to me has no end.

    In loneliness, I cry
    And look to You on high,
    With eyes fixed on Your face.
    I know I'll win this race!
    With You, I am a conqueror.

—Annette Carter, age eighteen

Ebenezer Stone: Choose a small, smooth stone and write the word *identity* on it. Place the stone where you will see it and remember that your identity is in God. He loves you and accepts you just the way you are.

IDENTITY: DAY 1

Parable: Tin Soldiers and Sheep

TIN SOLDIERS IN RED COATS AND FURRY BLACK HATS MARCHED IN military formation down a grassy slope. Their arms stiffly rose and fell, and their legs lifted straight out, then down, out, then down. As they marched down the hill, they started to slip and fall, landing on top of one another, causing great confusion. Then a large hand reached down and swept them all away. With their identity as tin soldiers, they had thought their marching was purposeful and important, but they were simply scooped up and put in a toy soldiers' box and left in the darkness and stillness. The grassy slope was now clear, peaceful, and quiet.

A little sheep bounced happily up the slope—nibbling on the grass, carefree and joyful. The Shepherd approached the sheep, staff in hand, and picked him up in His arms. The sheep snuggled close to the Shepherd and felt His warmth, kindness, and encouragement. The Shepherd carried the little sheep to the top of the hill, where they could see all around. The Shepherd could see everything that would happen in the future, but the little sheep was content to see only the Shepherd. He had no concerns about anything to come, because his Shepherd cared for him.

They sat together on the mountaintop. The sheep rested, and the Shepherd watched for danger, protecting the little sheep. They were content together. The Shepherd said to the little sheep, "Learn the discipline of rest so that in the midst of the intensity you do not break down physically or in any other way. Discipline yourself to rest, to enjoy nonproductivity and time with your family. I will guide you on this journey of rest and renewal. Do not seek activity that you think of as renewing but is really just another form of busyness. I am with you and am guiding you on My paths—both the paths of exciting ministry and the paths of quietness and restful renewal. Trust Me as you learn lessons of inactivity and quietness that I have prepared for you."

As the little sheep rested, he gained encouragement and strength from his Shepherd, secure in his identity as the Shepherd's beloved sheep.

Personal Reflection

Do you have toy soldiers on the hill of your life—busy things you do that accomplish little? Is your identity in what you accomplish? God is calling you to be His little sheep, to spend time in His presence, sit with Him, and let Him protect you, guide you, and encourage you. Rest in Him in quietness and trust.

Write your thoughts here.

Bible Verses

> Know that the Lord is God. It is he who made us, and we are his; we are his people, the sheep of his pasture. (Psalm 100:3)

> For anyone who enters God's rest also rests from their works, just as God did from his. (Hebrews 4:10)

Prayer Activities

- Listen for five or ten minutes to instrumental music that helps you rest. Here, for example, https://www.youtube.com/watch?v=Xx1MjhzKcYw is some soaking music.

- While you listen, doodle below with a pencil or colored pencils.

- When you are finished doodling, listen to what God is saying to you about your identity as His sheep. Write it here.

IDENTITY: DAY 2

Insight: Dots and Stars

In Max Lucado's children's book *You Are Special*,[1] little wooden people walked around town giving one another golden star stickers if they were successful or beautiful and gray dot stickers if they failed to succeed or please. Punchinello received only gray dot stickers because he was not attractive or talented like others, and he failed so often. He avoided people with many stars because he felt inferior. Then he met another wooden person named Lucia, who had neither dots nor stars. When he asked for her secret, she simply said he should go visit Eli, the woodcarver who had created them. Punchinello learned from Eli that it didn't matter what others thought about him—whether good or bad. The only opinion that really mattered was Eli's, because he was their maker. When Punchinello realized this might be true even for him, one of his dots fell to the ground.

If others' opinions are highly significant to us, we can be swayed by their position, their wealth (or lack of it), their looks, their with-it-ness, or their social adeptness. Often, we are the opposite of Punchinello but just as needy. We like to hang around people with lots of "stars" so others will think we have more stars as well. And if we are near people with lots of "dots," we fear others will think we are part of that less-than-illustrious crowd.

Subtly, we can desire to be the best, the most respected, or even the most revered. When we seek that, however, we are seeking to be a god. This is dangerous, for only God is the best, the most respected, and the one who deserves reverence. We must learn to live in the confidence of knowing we are created by God and He greatly values all people.

Picture hundreds of people in a sunny, grassy field, all holding hands and laughing for joy. They surge forward as one, helping one another in the joyful dance toward the goal. Their eyes are on the goal—Jesus. They do not think about which of them is the strongest or the best, for they are all as one. All support and balance each other. No person in the dance is either worshipped or despised, for all have their eyes on Jesus and are consumed by worship for Him. Leaders, encouragers, plodders, forceful ones, gentle ones, and wounded ones are all part of the joyful surge, hand in hand, toward the goal.

Personal Reflection

Are you swayed by people's opinions of you? Do you long for the approval of those around you? Do you secretly look down on certain people and envy others? God is inviting you to spend time with Him and listen to what He thinks of you. He would love for you to see life as a joyful dance toward Jesus, with everyone encouraging one another and keeping their eyes on Him.

Write your thoughts here.

Bible Verse

> "Teacher," they said, "we know that you are a man of integrity and that you teach the way of God in accordance with the truth. You aren't swayed by others, because you pay no attention to who they are." (Matthew 22:16)

Prayer Activities

- Take time to pray this prayer now.

  Lord, help me not to be swayed by people's opinions of me. Help me be like You in everything I do and live like You and for You, with Your opinion being the only one that really counts. Help me see myself as one whom You love and esteem equally with all others. Help me live with a pure heart in obedience and worship to You so I never cause You sadness or pain but bring You joy. And please help me love and encourage others with Your genuine love.

- What do you sense God is saying to you in response? (Write it below.)

- Ask God to give you a picture of what He thinks of you. Then draw it in the space below.

IDENTITY: DAY 3

Life Story: The Performer

I SAT ALONE BACKSTAGE. MY PERFORMING ACT WAS OVER, MAKEUP mask washed off and costume tossed to the side. Lonely and vulnerable, I ached to feel God's love for the real me, not just the masked performer.

The stage was my life as a young pastor's wife in downtown Toronto. The mask was the smile I painted on my face to cover up my pain and insecurity. The costume was my attempt to look and dress right, to be credible in my role. My act was the flourish of activities I performed, craving acceptance from others and ultimately from God.

Then one day, the curtain closed in my heart. I realized that though the song and dance, bright lights, and applause of people invigorated and flattered me, the performer was not me. It was a well-developed facade. The real me was maskless, costume-less, and alone, afraid to be seen for who I was and longing to feel truly loved by God.

I did not feel worthy unless I proved myself, performed with excellence, and made God proud to be my Father. I knew God's love was unconditional, but I could not feel it. How could God love me, so full of imperfections and insecurities?

Yearning to prove God's unconditional love for me, I sat down on our living room couch with my Bible and a sheet of paper. Starting in Genesis, I wrote down every reference I could find of God's love for people throughout the Bible.

I discovered anew that God's love for me was faithful and everlasting. Knowing me before I was born, He formed me and knit me together to be me. I realized I had believed the lie that I must perform to be worthy, loved, and accepted. Because of this, I could not feel God's unconditional love.

I admitted that the empty glitter of performing and masking myself was worthless, destructive, and alienating. I then declared that because God loved me, He accepted me, changed me, and used me. He taught me to accept myself and reach out to others. My heart's cry was for God to help me feel His love, live unmasked, and obey Him, and not to perform an empty, futile show. I asked Him to help me to live secure, comforted, and unafraid and to feel accepted and worthwhile in His unfailing love.

God met me in an unforgettable way that day as I prayed, "I reach out to You, God. My heart is breaking. I need so desperately to feel Your love. I look up with tear-filled eyes and see Your arms lovingly reaching out to hold me. Your tender eyes accept me as me. You have been waiting and waiting for me to come home to Your warm embrace. I am home, I am safe, I am me, in my Father's loving arms."

Personal Reflection

Do you ever feel like a performer, trying to look like a true follower of God but wondering if He accepts you as you are? God loves you just the way you are, and His love for you will never, ever end. No matter how much you disappoint Him, He will always love you. Take time now to thank Him for loving you and making you the way you are.

Write your thoughts here.

Bible Verses

> "Though the mountains be shaken and the hills be removed, yet my unfailing love for you will not be shaken nor my covenant of peace be removed," says the LORD, who has compassion on you. (Isaiah 54:10)

> The LORD appeared to us in the past, saying: "I have loved you with an everlasting love; I have drawn you with unfailing kindness." (Jeremiah 31:3)

Prayer Activities

- Ask God to speak to you now, telling you how He sees you. Write what you sense He is saying.

- Write a prayer of thanks to God for His love for you and acceptance of you.

- Write Isaiah 54:10 or Jeremiah 31:3 on a piece of paper and stick it on a mirror in your home. Whenever you look in the mirror, thank God that His love for you is unconditional and never ending.

IDENTITY: DAY 4

Insight: The Painting

In *The Return of the Prodigal Son*, Henri Nouwen says, "I am constantly surprised at how I keep taking the gifts God has given me—my health, my intellectual and emotional gifts—and keep using them to impress people, receive affirmation and praise, and compete for rewards, instead of developing them for the glory of God."[2] Many of us, like Nouwen, are highly motivated by human praise and rewards. When we do something praiseworthy, we feel good about ourselves. When we fail, we feel useless, inadequate, and unlovable.

We can learn from Jesus to be humble. He showed His humility by coming to earth to serve people who were selfish and egotistical. He left the sinless perfection of heaven to sacrifice Himself for ungrateful, undeserving people. He lived a life of perfect humility.

Humble people realize they are helpless and unimportant apart from God. When others praise them, they don't bask in the glory, for the glory is God's. And when others don't notice them, they have not suddenly become useless, for their standing with God remains unchanged.

Because of this, we must not yearn for recognition by others or long for positions of prominence or prestige. We are not more special or noteworthy to God than others, no matter how menial or untalented they may seem. Neither are we less important than the most respected leader. From the lowliest servant to the greatest leader, all are equally noteworthy in God's eyes. In fact, the truly greatest leaders have the hearts and hands of lowly servants.

In all this, our heart attitude is key. We are called to be humble servants of the great King and to accomplish His plan, for His glory. True humility is being faithful and loyal to Jesus, seeking no honor and recognition for ourselves.

When we are humble, our greatest desire is for God to be praised. When people look at an exquisite painting, they don't say, "Oh, painting, you are so beautiful. Thank you for displaying your colors so brilliantly. Thank you for bringing me much joy." Instead, they comment on the beauty, perhaps on how the painting stirs their emotions, then praise the artist who combined simple colors with great skill and much time and produced a masterpiece. In the same way, we don't walk up to a beautiful flower garden and say, "Flowers, you are so beautiful." Instead, we praise the gardener, the one who planted and tends the flowers. And we don't thank a musical instrument for playing so skillfully. The musician deserves the praise.

We are like paintings, flowers, and musical instruments. May all praise for the beauty seen in us and the good done through us go completely to God. And may He help us develop our gifts for His glory.

Personal Reflection

Are you willing to lay down your pride and selfishness at the feet of Jesus and be truly humble? When Jesus did amazing things, the people praised God. Are you willing to give God the praise for the good things you accomplish?

Write your thoughts here.

Bible Verses

> The Lord was with Joseph and gave him success in whatever he did. (Genesis 39:23)

> The people were amazed when they saw the mute speaking, the crippled made well, the lame walking and the blind seeing. And they praised the God of Israel. (Matthew 15:31)

> But whatever were gains to me I now consider loss for the sake of Christ. What is more, I consider everything a loss because of the surpassing worth of knowing Christ Jesus my Lord. (Philippians 3:7–8)

Prayer Activities

- What are some things you do well? List them here and praise God for these abilities.

- Ask God what He wants to say to you about your abilities and write what you sense He is saying.

- Find some pictures in magazines or online that represent things you enjoy doing or would like to learn to do. Make a collage with them. Whenever you look at the collage, praise God for His faithfulness and help in empowering you to do these things for Him.

IDENTITY: DAY 5

Parable: Belonging

JESUS'S FRIENDS ENTERED A STILL FOREST WITH TALL TREES AND little light. They felt hesitant to be there, but Jesus wanted them to enter. Looking up, they saw warm yellow sunlight at the top of the trees. They felt encouraged because they knew Jesus was with them. He was shining His blessing on them even though the warmth of His blessing didn't quite reach them in the dense forest.

They felt the presence of vicious wild animals and heard their growls. When they stopped in fear, they saw evil eyes shining through the undergrowth. They felt alone and afraid, but they knew Jesus was with them because He had guided them there. The evil animals skulked in the underbrush but did not come near to harm Jesus's friends because of His presence. Then a shaft of light shone down on them, and their fear left as they felt Jesus's presence more strongly than the fear. They felt safe and comforted.

Jesus led them to a path that was smooth and clear, with soft dirt under their feet. They found it much easier to walk now that they were out of the brambly thickness of the pathless forest undergrowth.

They walked along the path with lighter hearts. Up ahead, they saw a clearing and heard voices of people laughing and talking together. They ran toward the people because they longed to be with others who followed Jesus. When they arrived, Jesus's other friends embraced them and welcomed them into their great celebration. Each one belonged there, and they sang and danced together in a long line, praising Jesus in a curving, twirling worship dance.

Each person held a beautiful red flower with roots still on the stem in one hand and a cup of clear, pure water in the other. Each received Jesus's blessing, moving forward on the path as Jesus led them. They walked with their hands joined, helping one another carry the water and flowers.

Then Jesus brought them to an open field. He instructed them to plant their flowers in the fertile soil and water them with the cups of water. Each person planted and watered a flower in the sunny, spacious meadow beside the forest. The flowers grew and flourished. They joined the planters in lifting their faces and singing praises to God. And they all sang a new song of praise.

Jesus's friends no longer felt alone. They were in community, worshipping God with their many new friends and companions. They thanked God for His goodness to them and for their sense of belonging with others in community.

Personal Reflection

Perhaps you identify yourself as a child of God, but do you identify with a group of His followers? He invites us to join Him in community with others to praise Him, to grow in fellowship, and to serve others.

Write your thoughts here.

Bible Verses

> In Christ we, though many, form one body, and each member belongs to all the others. We have different gifts, according to the grace given to each of us.
>
> If your gift is prophesying, then prophesy in accordance with your faith; if it is serving, then serve; if it is teaching, then teach; if it is to encourage, then give encouragement; if it is giving, then give generously; if it is to lead, do it diligently; if it is to show mercy, do it cheerfully.
>
> Love must be sincere. Hate what is evil; cling to what is good. Be devoted to one another in love. Honor one another above yourselves. (Romans 12:5–10)

Prayer Activities

- What community of faith-filled people do you identify with? What group(s) do you belong to?

- Write a prayer to God, thanking Him for those people. If you feel alone, ask Him to give you a community of people to join.

- Which of the gifts in Romans 12:5–10 (above) has God given you?

- How can you use your gift(s) to serve others?

IDENTITY: DAY 6

Prayer and Reflection

GOD CARES ABOUT OUR IDENTITY! HE KNOWS US AND LOVES US JUST the way we are.

In the spaces below, write who you are, what you like to do, and what you don't like to do.

- Who I Am

- What I Like to Do

- What I Don't Like to Do

Thank God for each thing you've written above and ask Him to help you grow closer to Him and be used by Him in each area.

Listen to the song "You Say" by Lauren Daigle. Doodle here while you listen to the song. https://www.youtube.com/watch?v=sIaT8Jl2zpI

What is God saying to you?

Look back over the past week on this devotional journey. Write at least one thing you would like to remember from the week.

WEEK 4

Tears of Thanksgiving

Give thanks to the Lord, for he is good;
his love endures forever. Let the redeemed of the Lord tell their
story—Let them give thanks to the Lord for his unfailing love
and his wonderful deeds for mankind.

—Psalm 107:1-2, 8

This week, we will practice the art of thanksgiving. Thankfulness brightens our eyes, lifts our spirits, calms our worries, and gives us joy. Let's thank Him for what He has done—for His good gifts to us.

My Cry

Falling leaves, falling tears,
    Falling,
        Falling autumn season.
Barren trees, lonely hearts
    Crying,
        Crying, "Where's the reason?"
Chilling winds, aching sobs
    Piercing,
        Piercing hush-filled air.
Fading flowers, dimming hopes,
    Sighing,
        Sighing, "No one cares!"

God's Response

Hush, my little child.
    Wipe away your tears.
Let the sounds of dusk
    Penetrate your ears.
Birds and crickets sing
    Nighttime songs of praise.
Darkness cannot hush
    The joyful songs they raise.
Oh, my lonely child,
    Listen now and learn.
Thankfulness and praise
    Make your joy return.
Crickets do not worry.
    Songbirds never fear.
Rest, my little one.
    Trust Me. I am here!

—Annette Carter, age eighteen

Ebenezer Stone: Choose a small, smooth stone and write the word *thanksgiving* on it. Place the stone where you will see it and remember to thank God every day.

THANKSGIVING: DAY 1

Parable: The Field of Corn

A FIELD FLOURISHED WITH CORNSTALKS THAT WERE RICH, GREEN, and tall, reaching up into the sunny, clear blue sky. The corn was ripe—plump and large, ready to be picked. The wind gently touched the leaves and corn tassels. Full of life and vibrancy, the corn plants celebrated because their work was almost done. The corn would soon be harvested and taken to nourish many.

The corn plants remembered a number of months previous when they were just seeds. The hard winter's frosty winds chilled the few naked cornstalks left in the barren ground after the harvest. The frozen, unyielding ground seemed suffocated under the pressure of the blanketing snow. There was no hope, no life, just the barrenness of death. But there was also rest—a deep rest for the soil that had worked so hard through the growing season. But it wasn't a green pasture kind of rest. More of a frigid grave.

Then a soft spring wind started blowing. The sun leaned toward the soil to embrace it once again. Warmth enveloped the frozen ground and softened it. Gentle rains and new life stirred the soil. Then the Farmer ploughed the ground and planted the seeds.

The seeds waited in the darkness of the rich, fertile soil, slowly changing and growing in that hidden place. Finally, they poked their green shoots into the waiting, welcoming rays of sunshine. They grew and developed in the glorious summer months, anticipating the harvest.

Then harvest time arrived. There was great rejoicing as the harvesters gathered the long-awaited cobs of corn. Winter would come again, for such are the seasons, but the harvest was plentiful. Seeds would be saved to plant once again, to produce more life after the cold quietness of winter. So the flourishing corn plants clapped for joy, raising their leaves in thanks to God. There was great thanksgiving because the harvest had finally come.

Personal Reflection

Whatever season you are in, God is there. No matter how long and cold the winter season, there is hope, for spring will always come. And no matter how long the growing season lasts, one day the harvest will come, and with it a time of great thanksgiving!

Write your thoughts here.

Bible Verses

> Let us not become weary in doing good, for at the proper time we will reap a harvest if we do not give up. (Galatians 6:9)

> So then, just as you received Christ Jesus as Lord, continue to live your lives in him, rooted and built up in him, strengthened in the faith as you were taught, and overflowing with thankfulness. (Colossians 2:6–7)

Prayer Activities

- What season are you in right now?[3]

    o Is it winter, with little joy, no fruit, and coldness in your soul? Thank God for this time to withdraw in the quietness and focus on Him, deepening your relationship with Him in the stillness.
    o Is it spring, with fresh signs of hope and change to come? Thank God for this season of new growth in areas that were previously bare and unproductive.
    o Is it summer, with much growth, productivity, and evidence of blessing? Thank God for this time of active, life-giving, flourishing work and ministry.
    o Is it fall, a time of rich harvest and enjoying the fruit of your labor? Thank God for this joyous time of harvest as you release your fruit and allow it to be planted and grow into independent plants.

- Write a prayer to God, thanking Him for the season you are in. What blessings of this season can you thank Him for? Write them in your prayer below.

Thank You, Lord, for this season of ...

Thank You that ...

THANKSGIVING: DAY 2

Life Story: God Cares

Before we moved to Hungary as International Workers with the Alliance Canada, I often felt joyless and worried. Because I was a child of God, I believed my life should be characterized by joy and peace, but I couldn't seem to find it. Even the prospect of experiencing Hungary didn't really excite me, although I knew God was sending us there. I felt overwhelmed as I thought of the many new things we would encounter and the challenges we would face as we moved there with our eighteen-month-old daughter, Stephanie. I prayed for God to somehow fill me with His joy and peace.

The day we left for Hungary, a song started playing in my head about putting on a garment of praise instead of the spirit of heaviness and about choosing to exalt God. I discovered the song was based on Isaiah 61:1–3, which says,

> The Spirit of the Sovereign Lord is on me, because the Lord has anointed me to proclaim good news to the poor. He has sent me to bind up the brokenhearted, to proclaim freedom for the captives and release from darkness for the prisoners, to proclaim the year of the Lord's favor and the day of vengeance of our God, to comfort all who mourn, and provide for those who grieve in Zion—to bestow on them a crown of beauty instead of ashes, the oil of joy instead of mourning, and a garment of praise instead of a spirit of despair. They will be called oaks of righteousness, a planting of the Lord for the display of his splendor.

These verses became my commissioning promises as we left for our new adventure. As I sang the words to the song, I began to learn one of the secrets to joy: praising and thanking God, even when my heart is heavy.

Our plane arrived in Budapest at 9:30 p.m. Little Stephanie was restless for much of the flight, so when the flight attendant announced she was turning off the lights, I wondered wearily if the plane was out of fuel and they were trying to conserve energy. Then I gazed out the window and realized what was happening. With the plane's cabin lights off, we could see Budapest's millions of lights sparkling in the darkness below. I felt numb as I looked down. "So what? Another large city. What's the big deal?"

Then I saw the shadowy Danube River bisecting the city, with majestic bridges like diamond-studded bracelets on a long, slender arm. I recognized some of the bridges from pictures we had seen, and my heart beat faster. This wasn't just any city; this was Budapest, the beautiful capital of Hungary, our new home! Something awakened in me as I soaked in the beauty of the scene below. God was answering my prayer and filling my heart with joy and thanksgiving.

When the plane landed, we had no one to meet us at the busy Budapest airport. We ordered train tickets in stumbling, travel guide Hungarian and traveled to eastern Hungary, where we would study the language. When our train arrived at our destination, we saw all the tracks between our platform and the main station. We realized we somehow needed to maneuver our three large suitcases, oversized duffel bag, two carry-ons, baby stroller, and eighteen-month-old Stephanie down all the stairs to the underpass and up again to the station. As we stood there wondering what to do, a lady asked us in German if she could assist us. In my faltering high school German, I explained our predicament. Her husband generously helped carry our heavy bags, despite the August heat.

God was saying, "You are My children, and I am taking care of you. Do not be afraid!" He gave us joy in knowing He cared for us with an even deeper love than we loved our sweet Stephanie. And our hearts filled with thanks to Him.

Personal Reflection

Do you see yourself as God's beloved child? When life is stressful, remember He loves you and cares for you far more deeply than a parent with their own child. He comforts you, provides for you, and fills you with joy and purpose. And He invites you to thank Him in every circumstance!

Write your thoughts here.

Bible Verses

> "As a mother comforts her child, I will comfort you." (Isaiah 66:13)

> Give thanks in all circumstances; for this is God's will for you in Christ Jesus. (1 Thessalonians 5:18)

Prayer Activities

- What ways do caring parents show love to their children?

- How has God shown love to you in these ways? Thank Him for His love.

THANKSGIVING: DAY 3

Parable: The Road of Renewal

JESUS'S FRIENDS WALKED ON A DRY AND DUSTY ROAD THAT WAS DEEPLY rutted, uneven, and hard to travel. On both sides of the road stood dry, limp trees and bushes. Everything was dry—the road, the vegetation, everything.

The wearying road looked like it would never change. In the distant past, it had been smooth and vibrant, bordered by life-giving trees and flowers. But over time, this path of beauty and refreshing had become dry and lifeless.

Then God's Spirit hovered over the road like a cloud of glory. He sent refreshing rains to the dry and hardened ground, softening the path and preparing for tender grass to carpet the way. Renewing springs and cool rain prepared the ground beside the path for new growth and life.

Then a great river swept down the road, quickly and effortlessly carrying everything along with it. The roadway became a refreshing riverway that brought life to the vegetation all around. Bushes, trees, and flowers grew up beside the river. New life and hope sprang up and multiplied, bringing life, fruitfulness, and growth all along the river and spreading far beyond.

Jesus's friends flowed with the river and heard Him say, "Prepare now for a season of great refreshing and growth ahead. I am doing a new thing among you. Do you not perceive it? I am making dry places vibrant with life and growth. My Spirit is upon each of you, and I am bringing new life and hope to all who are willing to follow Me with all their heart. Submit yourselves to Me. Take up your cross and follow Me, and I will bring life and refreshing to your souls and growth and renewal to the church. I am at work in you and among you, for My glory."

Jesus's friends' hearts overflowed with thanksgiving to God for the new life He was creating. They thanked Him for His promise to refresh them and those around them.

Personal Reflection

Have you been trudging along a dry, uneven roadway, with little life in and around you—tired and stressed? Maybe in recent months you've noticed a lack of growth and vibrancy. But God is doing a new thing, bringing new growth and life by His Spirit. He invites you to ask Him to renew you. His river will sweep you up and carry you wherever He wants you to go, bringing life to you and those around you. He invites you to thank Him for the new thing He is doing.

Write your thoughts here.

Bible Verses

> Forget the former things; do not dwell on the past. See, I am doing a new thing! Now it springs up; do you not perceive it? I am making a way in the desert and streams in the wasteland. (Isaiah 43:18–19)

Prayer Activities

- What new things is God doing in your life right now? How is God making a way in your desert spaces and streams in your wasteland?

- Write a prayer of thanks to God for healing you and for bringing new vibrancy to your life.

- What do you sense God is saying to you right now?

- Use markers or colored pencils to write Isaiah 43:18–19 (above) on a piece of paper to put on your wall as a reminder to thank Him for doing a new thing in you.

THANKSGIVING: DAY 4

Life Story: I Will Trust You

Our son Daniel was born at the end of our first year of Hungarian language study in eastern Hungary. As I woke up each night and sat in my rocking chair nursing him, I struggled with a terrible fear of evil.

I prayed against any spiritual forces coming against me, but the fear would not leave. I couldn't understand why. I felt like the blackness of the night was engulfing me, and I would soon be overcome.

The words of Psalm 23 comforted me: "The Lord is my Shepherd. I shall not be in want ... Even though I walk through the valley of the shadow of death, I will fear no evil, for you are with me." I knew God was with me, but I couldn't feel His presence and peace. I didn't know why God was allowing these horrible attacks of fear against me. I wondered if I would ever be released from this nightly terror and be at peace again.

But I knew God was teaching me to trust Him—to trust that He was in control and would never allow the battle to overcome me. Even as I held my infant Daniel in my arms in that dark room and he couldn't see me, God was holding me in His loving arms in the darkness of my fear, and He comforted me. I chose to trust Him, for He was good. He was in control.

As I gave my fears to God, I thanked Him that although He did not promise a life free from evil attacks, He did promise He would rescue me from them. I thanked Him for His protection and chose to trust Him.

A year later, we moved to northwestern Hungary. As I sat with God one day, I wrote this prayer:

> Lord, thank You for this amazing sense of Your peace, which is greater, perhaps, than at any time in my life. Help me not to fear dark times will come again when I will struggle to live in joy and power. Thank You that because of those risks, I must keep clinging to You.

On sunny, clear days, I ride high on Your shoulders. I clap my hands and sing for joy as You carry me through unfamiliar, exciting territory. You guide my willing hands, skillfully working through them, and You delight in my delight at Your creativity.

Feeling the gentle breeze caress my face, I close my eyes, stretch up my hands in the warm rays of the sun, and shout with joy, "All is well! Thank the Lord! He is good!"

When heavy rain beats down on me, when I am cold and wet, and darkness oppresses me, I put my arms around Your neck and cling to You for warmth and protection. I hide my face in Your chest so the pelting rain won't sting me. Dark clouds close in around me, and the wind whips the clothes on my back, but I am not afraid. You are much stronger than I am and will carry me through the storm.

I snuggle close to You and learn from Your heartbeat and Your gentle whisper in my ear. My feeble voice is not unheard. It cuts like lightning through the storm: "All is well! Thank the Lord! He is good!"

Personal Reflection

When you are afraid, remember God loves you deeply and will deliver you from every evil attack. As you trust Him and thank Him for His goodness, He will fill your heart with peace.

Write your thoughts here.

Bible Verses

The Lord will rescue me from every evil attack and will bring me safely to his heavenly kingdom. To him be glory for ever and ever. Amen. (2 Timothy 4:18)

You will keep in perfect peace those whose minds are steadfast, because they trust in you. (Isaiah 26:3)

Prayer Activities

- What do you fear today?

- Give your fears to God and thank Him for His peace.

- Write things you thank God for despite your fears.

THANKSGIVING: DAY 5

Parable: The Jewels

JESUS TOOK HIS FRIEND TO A CAVE. PRICELESS BLUE SAPPHIRES SHONE brightly in the darkness, but the precious stones seemed meaningless and valueless to her. She felt she didn't need the pretty, shiny rocks, even if they were highly valuable. And she didn't like dark caves. She loved the beauty of nature, outside in the sunshine—in the fields, near flowers and pools of water.

"Take the jewels and value them," said Jesus.

She picked up the jewels in both hands.

"Now eat them," said Jesus.

As she swallowed them, the jewels became rays of light that burst within her and shone out of her. Each of the jewels, the valuable things that she personally didn't see the point in, became a beam of light for others.

She asked Jesus to help her be thankful for all He had given her, even the things she didn't see personal value in. She asked for strength to accept all the jewels of her work that in many ways seemed personally valueless to her. And she invited Him to use the light from those things to shine through her and light the way for many others.

Jesus then took her on a journey back to her childhood. He flooded each part of her past with light—showing her the great joys and blessings of each season of her life. Each one was a jewel of light. Her heart filled with thanksgiving as they journeyed through her life and gathered the jewels.

Jesus added each jewel of light to an exquisite robe of beauty that He gave her. She put on the robe and danced in praise to Him. As He flooded her with light, she felt great beauty and grace, and her heart filled with thanksgiving.

Personal Reflection

Are there things in your life that God has given you to do or care for, or experiences you've gone through, that you do not truly value? Thank God for each one and ask for His help to value them as He does. Take time to reflect on your life and thank God for each of the joys and blessings He has given you throughout the years.

Write your thoughts here.

Bible Verses

> Give thanks to the Lord, for he is good.
> His love endures forever …
> He remembered us in our low estate
> His love endures forever.
> and freed us from our enemies.
> His love endures forever.
> He gives food to every creature.
> His love endures forever.
> Give thanks to the God of heaven.
> His love endures forever.
> (Psalm 136:1, 23–26)

Prayer Activities

- As you think back to all the good things that have happened in your life and all the blessings you have received from God, choose several and create a psalm in the spaces below.

    Give thanks to the Lord, for He is good.
    His love endures forever.

    He ...
    His love endures forever.

    And ...
    His love endures forever.

    He ...
    His love endures forever.

    And ...
    His love endures forever.

    He ...
    His love endures forever.

    And ...
    His love endures forever.

    Give thanks to the God of heaven.
    His love endures forever.

- Pray the psalm out loud, thanking God for each blessing.

THANKSGIVING: DAY 6

Prayer and Reflection

GOD INVITES US TO THANK HIM NOT ONLY FOR BIG SPIRITUAL blessings but also for the everyday blessings all around us.

Give thanks to God for one hundred things!

1–10   Look around you right now. What are ten things you see that you are thankful for? Write them below and thank God for them.

11–20   Now look out the window. Write ten more things you are thankful for.

21–30   Go to a different room or place. Write ten more things you are thankful for.

31–40   Think about your family and friends. Write ten people you are thankful for.

41–50   Think about your church or community. Write ten things you are thankful for.

51–60   Think about your work. Write ten work-related things you are thankful for.

61–70   Think about your hobbies. Write ten more things you are thankful for.

71–80   Think about foods you like. Write ten kinds of food you are thankful for.

81–90   Think about flowers and plants. Write ten kinds you are thankful for.

91–100 Think about your town or city. Write ten more things you are thankful for!

Look back over the past week on this devotional journey. Write at least one thing you would like to remember from the week.

WEEK 5

Tears of Joy

The king rejoices in your strength, Lord. How great is his joy in the victories you give! Surely you have granted him unending blessings and made him glad with the joy of your presence.
—Psalm 21:1, 6

Weeping may stay for the night, but
rejoicing comes in the morning.
—Psalm 30:5b

Joy is lightness of heart, excitement in the soul. Unlike happiness, it does not require pleasantness or success. Instead, it is a choice to see the good in difficult circumstances, to be hopeful and positive when tempted to despair, and to trust in God with exuberance no matter what is happening. This week, we will explore the joy of choosing joy!

Come to Me

Are you war torn and weary?
Are you wounded and scarred?
Is the road that you're traveling
Uphill and hard?

Rest in my promise,
My hope that is true.
I save you, restore you.
I recreate you.

Rest in me fully.
Give me your fears.
I know all your struggles.
I gather your tears.

I'm going before you,
Preparing the way.
I love you. I'm for you!
I'm with you today.

Come, lay down your burdens.
Come, rest in my arms.
Come, trust in Me fully.
Do not be alarmed.

Come, enter My presence,
I'll quiet the noise.
Release all your sorrows.
Receive all My joys!

Ebenezer Stone: Choose a small, smooth stone and write the word *joy* on it. Place the stone where you will see it and remember to choose joy every day, no matter what happens.

JOY: DAY 1

Parable: Throne Room Joy

Jesus's friends climbed a pure white hill. They were an exuberant group of men, women, and children, all clothed in white. They felt a sense of buoyancy, expectation, and great joy as they sang, chattered, and laughed, anticipating seeing Jesus in His glory. As they approached the top, they saw a great fiery light everywhere. It opened up before them, and they entered a large throne room that was pure white and filled with dazzling light. The chamber reverberated with their joyful sounds.

Jesus rushed down from the throne to greet these friends whom He loved. They surrounded Him, and He hugged them and laughed with them. He wore a brilliant white robe and a huge smile, and His eyes shone with joy and warmth. As they crowded around Jesus, He loved, hugged, and welcomed each of them individually, all at once. He laughed and danced with them and spoke words that were like honey—sweet, smooth, and life-giving.

They all sat down around Him in the center of the great throne room, and He spoke words and stories of truth, power, life, and hope. Pure white doves of peace flowed from His words and rested upon each of them and absorbed into them. Then soft red hearts of love flowed to them from His words, and then golden keys of wisdom. After this, crystal glasses of clean water came from His words and rested in their hands. The glasses were full of compassion to be poured out on the needy—cups of cold water to be given in His name.

Then they all stood up with a great shout, linking their arms. They rose with Jesus into the clear blue sky—like a great, shining cloud alive with praise-filled adults and children, each overflowing with joy and excitement from being with Jesus.

Jesus chose different places for each to serve. He sent them to offer His water of compassion to needy people and bring them to Him. And He filled each with great joy as they let Him pour His love through them and as they lifted their hearts in joyful praise.

Personal Reflection

Do you realize that Jesus longs for you to be close to Him and rejoice in Him? He longs to give you His peace, love, and wisdom. He invites you to accept His cup of compassion and pour it out on other people so they also will come to Him. Will you ask Him to fill you with His compassion and joy today?

Write your thoughts here.

Bible Verses

> And giving joyful thanks to the Father, who has qualified you to share in the inheritance of his holy people in the kingdom of light. (Colossians 1:12)

> Shout for joy to the Lord, all the earth.
> Worship the Lord with gladness; come before him with joyful songs.
> Know that the Lord is God. It is he who made us, and we are his; we are his people, the sheep of his pasture.
> Enter his gates with thanksgiving and his courts with praise; give thanks to him and praise his name.
> For the Lord is good and his love endures forever;
> his faithfulness continues through all generations. (Psalm 100:1–5)

Prayer Activities

- Write Psalm 100 (above) as a prayer of joyful praise to God.

  I shout for joy to You, Lord. I worship You with gladness.

- Imagine you are in God's throne room and Jesus is welcoming you there, filling you with joy, and giving you cups of compassion for the needy. What would you like to say to Him now?

JOY: DAY 2

Life Story: Joy in San Marino

Some days, the weather in our life is mostly sunny—our relationships are peaceful, our bank accounts are adequate, and our work is going well. Other days, it is cloudy with boredom or looming problems. Still others, it is rainy with painful issues that we can't resolve, or it is stormy, and we are losing hope. How do we live as joyful people, whatever the weather?

One spring, while living in northeastern Hungary, I left my preschoolers with my husband for a few days so I could accompany a group of Hungarians on a short ministry trip to Italy, where my parents served. While there, we visited the tiny republic of San Marino, a quaint city-state built on a mountaintop.

As I sat on the mountain and savored our picnic, I enjoyed the beauty of the sunshine and the landscape below. The countryside lay before us like an intricate patchwork quilt of little towns and fields, beautifully bordered by the shimmering Adriatic Sea.

In the midst of my joy, I felt a pang of sadness that my family was not with me. But I realized that if they were, I would not be enjoying the view but would instead be running after my toddler to keep him from falling off the cliff. My joy could not be full, for I would miss either my family or the peaceful view.

I asked myself, "Can joy ever be truly complete, without something missing?" I concluded there is always a shadow of sadness when the light of earthly happiness is shining.

Then Psalm 16:11 came to mind, "You will fill me with joy in your presence, with eternal pleasures at your right hand." I realized the only place my joy can be full here on earth, and will one day be eternally full, is in God's presence. In His presence, I am completely bathed in His light and love. No shadows are cast on my soul, as from earthly happiness, for He is a consuming light that shines from every direction and leaves no shadow.

When I am in His presence and when I reflect on the eternal light of heaven, I experience fullness of joy.

That day on the mountain, I chose to focus my mind and heart on God. Even though my family was far away, I found my joy complete.

Personal Reflection

Are you learning to keep your eyes on Jesus and grow closer to Him, whether your life is bathed in sunshine, gray with clouds, soaked in rain, or blasted with storms? You can find joy in His presence, no matter what is going on within you or around you, because there is no darkness in Him, and He's the one who fills you with joy.

Write your thoughts here.

Bible Verses

> I keep my eyes always on the Lord. With him at my right hand, I will not be shaken.
> Therefore my heart is glad and my tongue rejoices; my body also will rest secure, because you will not abandon me to the realm of the dead, nor will you let your faithful one see decay.
> You make known to me the path of life; you will fill me with joy in your presence, with eternal pleasures at your right hand. (Psalm 16:8–11)

Prayer Activities

Take a few minutes to talk to God about the weather in your soul today.

- *Enter His presence.* Read Psalm 16:8–11 above and focus your mind on God. Remember that with Him you will not be shaken.
- *Tell God what you are feeling.* What is the weather in your soul today? Sunny with things going well? Cloudy with stress or boredom? Rainy with problems? Stormy and feeling out of control? Tell God about it.
- *Pray a scripture to Him.* Take a few minutes now to speak Zephaniah 3:14–17 as a prayer to God.

    > Sing, Daughter Zion; shout aloud, Israel! Be glad and rejoice with all your heart, Daughter Jerusalem! The Lord has taken away your punishment, he has turned back your enemy. The Lord, the King of Israel, is with you; never again will you fear any harm. On that day they will say to Jerusalem, "Do not fear, Zion; do not let your hands hang limp. The Lord your God is with you, the Mighty Warrior who saves. He will take great delight in you; in his love he will no longer rebuke you, but will rejoice over you with singing."

- *Choose joy.* Remember who you are—the child of your heavenly Father who delights in you and rejoices over you. Give Him all your stresses and problems and choose to rejoice in all the good things He has given you.

JOY: DAY 3

Insight: Count It Pure Joy

THE PROBLEMS WE FACE THROUGHOUT OUR DAY ARE NOT TRULY problems if we surrender those areas to Jesus. If we believe Christ is Lord, we will accept that everything coming into our day is permitted by Him and that He will work everything out for good (Romans 8:28). He invites us to "count it pure joy" when we "face trials of many kinds" (James 1:2) and to "do all things without grumbling or arguing" (Philippians 2:14).

When we surrender ourselves to Christ as Lord, we acknowledge that He is in control of all circumstances, even the disruptions and hard times. When our preschool child wakes up at 5:30 and won't go back to sleep, when the kids are fussy and uncooperative, when they don't sleep in the afternoon and we feel like we need a break, or when we have too many things to do and don't know which is most important, Jesus is still Lord. He gives us strength as we choose joy, because the joy of the Lord is our strength (Nehemiah 8:10).

If our life is a constant focus on our being comfortable and only doing distasteful things when we absolutely have to, then every difficult task, every interruption, every pile of dishes, and every piece of dirt or spill on the floor is unwanted—a burden, a stress. But when we deny our selfishness and do everything for God and for the sake of others, then even ironing can become a joy!

Difficulties in life are problems only if we haven't surrendered those areas to Jesus. If we give them to Him, they become challenges we can face with joy. In God's strength, we know the difficulties have come to us with His permission, for our benefit. And we therefore can live joyful, "problem-free" lives. As we choose joy and surrender to God, we find He loves us and gives us strength to do everything we need to do, even when we find it hard.

Personal Reflection

Do you have problems or tasks that make you wonder if God really sees you and cares about what you have to deal with? God loves you! Even when He allows hard things to happen to you or gives you difficult tasks to accomplish, He is shaping you into a more attractive, mature, faith-filled person.

Write your thoughts here.

Bible Verses

> Do not grieve, for the joy of the Lord is your strength. (Nehemiah 8:10)

> Whatever you do, work at it with all your heart, as working for the Lord, not for human masters, since you know that you will receive an inheritance from the Lord as a reward. It is the Lord Christ you are serving. (Colossians 3:23–24)

> Consider it pure joy, my brothers and sisters, whenever you face trials of many kinds, because you know that the testing of your faith produces perseverance. Let perseverance finish its work so that you may be mature and complete, not lacking anything. If any of you lacks wisdom, you should ask God, who gives generously to all without finding fault, and it will be given to you. (James 1:2–5)

Prayer Activities

- What tasks are hard for you? What problems are you facing that are stealing your joy? Write them here.

- Ask God to fill you with His pure joy in your trials and tasks and to help you do the things you don't like to do but need to get done.

- What do you sense He is saying to you now?

- What would you like to respond to Him?

JOY: DAY 4

Life Story: Where Is Joy?

When our daughter Stephanie was four and our son Daniel was two, we lived for a year in Kingston, Ontario, to connect with churches and share about our work in Hungary.

Perhaps you have read the children's book *Alexander and the Terrible, Horrible, No Good, Very Bad Day*.[4] Some days are like that. Even in Canada.

My "very bad day" started at breakfast when I sliced a cinnamon-raison bagel and the knife slipped, slicing my finger instead. After bandaging my wound, I headed to the grocery store. As I wheeled my cart through the fresh produce section, my watchband broke, and my watch crashed to the floor. I picked up the pieces, stuffed them in my purse, and then bought what I thought were seedless grapes. They weren't. They were full of slippery seeds that would have to be painstakingly removed, one by one, before I could give them to my preschoolers.

Because we were new in town, it was time for my first trip to a hairdresser. I sank into the chair and closed my eyes. Finally, I could relax. As the assistant lathered and rinsed my hair, I felt the tension of the morning wash away with the soapy suds.

The hairdresser pinned up a handful of my thick brown hair and started cutting the under-most layer. She froze. Gingerly, meticulously, she separated the strands as if looking for something. Then she called over another hairdresser, and they whispered in urgent tones.

When the hairdresser turned to me, her face was stiff, and she spoke with forced politeness. "There are nits in your hair, ma'am. Please buy some lice shampoo and treat your hair. I will quickly finish your haircut, but I can't dry and style it for you today. You are welcome to come back after a few weeks when the problem has been resolved."

I walked out of the hair salon feeling like I had a plague. I could imagine the bugs jeering at me as they hopped around my increasingly itchy head.

I drove home. After finding nits in my husband, Stephen's, hair, I checked Daniel's and found none. I called the school to have Stephanie's hair checked, but she was clear as well. Then I washed all our linens and asked Stephen to buy lice shampoo when he went out to pick up our computer that he had taken in for repairs. He came home and told me it had cost over $500 to fix the computer. I was aghast.

While I talked on the phone to my mother-in-law about the lice, little Daniel decided to get a job done on his own. He pulled off his very dirty diaper and put it neatly in the garbage can. Then he contentedly sat down to play here and there in his room, leaving dark stains all over his carpet and bed.

As I poured water in my glass at lunchtime, the lid fell off the container. Water gushed all over the table, my soup, the floor, and me. I cleaned up the mess and then ate cold, tasteless soup. After lunch, I lathered my hair with the lice shampoo and got in the shower to wash it off. There was no hot water!

Because we had been in transition from Hungary to Canada, Stephen and I hadn't been on a date in months. That evening, on our long-awaited date night, all I could think about was the lice in our hair laughing at us as we tried to enjoy our steak dinner!

Personal Reflection

Where is joy on days like this? We feel like jelly inside and want to cry or yell in frustration. We might feel like it's somehow our fault and we're not good enough. We have to make a choice between trying to run from the problems or giving them to God and trusting that His plans are good and He loves us deeply. Then, even the most "terrible, horrible, no good, very bad day" becomes an opportunity for joy!

Write your thoughts here.

Bible Verses

In all this you greatly rejoice, though now for a little while you may have had to suffer grief in all kinds of trials. These have come so that the proven genuineness of your faith—of greater worth than gold, which perishes even though refined by fire—may result in praise, glory and honor when Jesus Christ is revealed. (1 Peter 1:6–7)

Prayer Activities

- Say 1 Peter 1:6–7 as a prayer to God.

  Father, in all this I greatly rejoice...

- What do you sense God is saying to you? Write it here.

JOY: DAY 5

Parable: Heavy Burden

Jesus's friends came to Him with a heavy burden. He had called them to serve Him in a new location, and they feared the reports of cult groups and witchcraft there. They wondered what struggles and opposition they would face and felt like they were walking into a frightening, uncertain future. They had expected to be full of anticipation and joy in moving there, but instead they felt like a heavy weight had fallen on their shoulders.

The burden weighed so heavily on them that they brought it to Jesus. Holding the burden in their hands, they offered it up to Him.

"Here, Jesus. Please take this burden," they said. "It's too heavy for us to carry. Will You take it please?"

He took it from them, and they felt relieved.

But then He gave it back!

"Jesus, what are You doing?" they cried. "We gave You this burden because it was too heavy for us. Why are You giving it back? We can't bear it!"

Then they noticed His hands under theirs, bearing the weight of the burden.

He said to them, "I have given this burden, this ministry, into your hands. You are to work there and serve the people there. That's what I've called you to do. But I will bear the weight of the burden. I will work through your hands and give you the strength, power, and wisdom you need every day."

"Thank You, Jesus," they replied. "Thank You for Your promise, for Your support, and for bearing the weight of the burden that was too heavy for us to bear. And thank You for Your joy!"

Personal Reflection

Are you carrying a burden today that is too heavy for you? Do you feel weighed down with decisions, problems, or other stresses? If you release those issues to Jesus and let Him bear the weight of the burden, He will give you His peace and joy.

Write your thoughts here.

Bible Verses

> "Come to me, all you who are weary and burdened, and I will give you rest. Take my yoke upon you and learn from me, for I am gentle and humble in heart, and you will find rest for your souls. For my yoke is easy and my burden is light." (Matthew 11:28–30)

> Be joyful in hope, patient in affliction, faithful in prayer. (Romans 12:12)

> Cast all your anxiety on him because he cares for you. (1 Peter 5:7)

Prayer Activities

- What burdens are weighing on you today?

- Cup your palms before you and imagine you are carrying those burdens in your hands. Lift your hands up to Jesus and give your burdens to Him, remembering that though you may be weak and weighed down, He is strong, and His burden is light.

- Write Matthew 11:28–30 (above) as a prayer to Jesus:
  Jesus, I come to You. I am weary ...

- Write a prayer of thanks to God for bearing the weight of your burdens and giving you joy.

- What do you sense He is saying to you right now? Write it here.

JOY: DAY 6

Prayer and Reflection

Joy is a choice! Habakkuk wrote these verses from the difficulties in His agricultural context:

> Though the fig tree does not bud and there are no grapes on the vines, though the olive crop fails and the fields produce no food, though there are no sheep in the pen and no cattle in the stalls, yet I will rejoice in the Lord. I will be joyful in God my Savior.
>
> The Sovereign Lord is my strength; he makes my feet like the feet of a deer, he enables me to tread on the heights. (Habakkuk 3:17–19)

What difficulties are you facing today? Using Habakkuk's template above, write your own prayer to God, filling in the lines with situations from your life.

Though (negative thing) …

and (negative thing) …

though (negative thing) …

and (negative thing) …

though *(negative thing)* ...

and *(negative thing)* ...

yet I will rejoice in You, Lord. I will be joyful in You, God my Savior.

You, Sovereign Lord, are my strength.

You *(positive thing)* ...

You enable me to *(positive thing)* ...

Look back over the past week on this devotional journey. Write at least one thing you would like to remember from the week.

WEEK 6

Tears of Healing

Lord my God, I called to you for help, and you healed me.
—Psalm 30:2

Pray for each other so that you may be healed. The prayer of a righteous person is powerful and effective.
—James 5:16

Sometimes we think of healing as only physical. While that is an important aspect of healing, God wants to heal us in every way—physically, emotionally, mentally, spiritually, and relationally.

As we explore His healing this week, He invites us to come to Him and ask Him to heal us, believing He will do so in His way and timing.

Violated Lambs

For the many children (and adults) who need healing from abuse.

Little child, little lamb,
Sweet, innocent lamb
Crouched in pain,
Silent, inner pain.
Violated, cruelly ripped apart,
Bleeding to death
Inside, deep, deep inside.

Sunny childhood sweetness
Bitterly clutched and pawed away
By deathly touches,
Smooth embraces
That leave ripped-open wounds
Of inner turmoil.

Horror, helplessness, terror.
The bogeyman is real.
When will the pain go away?
When will the torture end?

Wounded child,
Curled in a tight ball
Of filth and guilt.
Stripped of innocence.
Alone, desperately alone.
Crying tears of bitter pain
From a dark well continually refilled
   With newer, viler pain.
Abandoned to suffer in silence.

No one cares for the
Wounded lamb,

Suffering a slow death
In darkness, grief,
   Inner turmoil.

Oh, Lamb of God!
Bruised, tortured, rejected, abused,
Assaulted by sinful men,
Come! Come heal Your lambs!
Heal their hearts, bind their wounds,
Speak comfort, hope, joy, victory.
Hold them close
   To Your wounded heart,
     That by Your stripes
      They may be healed.
Wash them whiter than snow.
Adorn them with beauty and honor.
Bring them wholeness,
   Complete healing.
Love them deeply, securely.
Embrace them with purity.
Restore to them their innocence.
Turn their darkness to sunshine,
Their despair to bright hope,
   Their bitter loneliness
     To the fullness
      Of Your complete acceptance
      And love.

Heal Your lambs, oh Lamb of God!
Heal Your lambs!

Ebenezer Stone: Choose a small, smooth stone and write the word *healing* on it. Place the stone where you will see it and remember to pray for God to heal others and yourself.

HEALING: DAY 1

Parable: The Good Shepherd and the Sheep

A TRAIL STRETCHED OUT BEFORE A SMALL, FLUFFY SHEEP AS SHE followed her Good Shepherd. As the little sheep walked, she saw many wounded sheep, dying or dead, beside the path. The broken sheep were her broken dreams, and she felt the ache of loss.

Then she saw God's great eagles sweep down to lift up the dead and wounded sheep. The eagles carried those broken dreams and disappointments to Jesus's empty tomb, where they sank into the floor, disintegrating into dust.

From the dust, multitudes of crimson roses grew up, filling the tomb with fragrance, beauty, and life. The roses floated out of the tomb and took root all along the path where the sheep followed Jesus. Now, instead of broken, wounded dreams beside the path, thousands of beautiful, fragrant roses of hope delighted her way.

As she continued following her Good Shepherd, thorns engulfed her path. These sins of herself and of those around her poked her flesh, hindered her progress, and caused tears of pain to spill from her eyes. Then her Shepherd lifted her and gently extracted the thorns. His tears bathed her wounds, soothing and healing them.

A fire suddenly erupted and consumed all the thorns. The Shepherd held His little sheep close and explained that the fire was the time of trial that was ravaging her peace and the peace of the world.

Then the wind swept up all the ashes. They swirled around her. She couldn't breathe, so she hid her face in His chest. She inhaled His goodness and His fragrance of joy and peace until the storm passed. Then the lush, velvety grass of His grace renewed the ground, and she could walk in freedom.

The Good Shepherd rose up, taller and greater, until He towered over everything. His little sheep saw huge armies below. Countless armor-clad soldiers on horses sang praises to God as they cantered toward a large battlefield. The great battle would be in the distant future, but the preparation was now. The little sheep saw her Good Shepherd holding each of His soldiers in His arms, even as He was holding her. And she praised Him.

Personal Reflection

Will you give Jesus your broken dreams and disappointments and allow Him to replace them with His beauty and hope? Do you have sins you need to confess? Will you allow the Good Shepherd to extract those thorns and heal you? And when the fire consumes the thorns, will you cling to Him, inhaling His goodness, joy, and peace? As you head into battle against evil, will you let our Good Shepherd hold you? Will you rest in His peace, even as you prepare for the battle? God is calling you to come to Him, your Good Shepherd, and find rest for your soul.

Write your thoughts here.

Bible Verses

> The Lord is my shepherd, I lack nothing. He makes me lie down in green pastures, he leads me beside quiet waters, he refreshes my soul. He guides me along the right paths for his name's sake.
> Even though I walk through the darkest valley, I will fear no evil, for you are with me; your rod and your staff, they comfort me.
> You prepare a table before me in the presence of my enemies. You anoint my head with oil; my cup overflows.
> Surely your goodness and love will follow me all the days of my life, and I will dwell in the house of the Lord forever. (Psalm 23:1–6)

Prayer Activities

- Pray the following prayer:

  Oh, Lord, please do this work of soul healing in me. Exchange my broken dreams for Your beauty and hope. Burn up the sin in and around me and heal my wounds. Hold me in Your arms even as You prepare me for battle, and give me rest. In Jesus's name. Amen.

- What do you sense God is saying to you in response to your prayer?

- Read Psalm 23 (above) and think about what you need most from your Good Shepherd today. Underline the phrases that stand out to you.

- Write a prayer or poem to Jesus, your Good Shepherd.

HEALING: DAY 2

Life Story: Wounded Healer

Years ago, I suffered the pain of conflict with a friend. As I processed her harsh words and accusations, I wrote this imagined dialogue between us in my journal:

> "Please let me love you," I said.
> *"Okay, have a try," she replied.*
> "I care about you, Friend," I said.
> *"But not enough."*—Stab!
> "I'd like to spend time with you," I said.
> *"But you don't spend enough," she replied.*
> "I'd like to grow to know you, love you more," I said.
> *"But you don't love me enough."*—Stab!
> "You can grow deeper in God, love others with His love," I said.
> *"But they don't love me enough. And neither do you."*—Stab!

I wondered if the problem was with me. Perhaps I was full of empty promises, empty dreams, empty expectations, and empty hopes in my empty, tear-filled heart.

I thought people were lovely. They stank like dirty sheep. I sought for the good in them. They stabbed me in the heart. From my broken heart bled neither poison nor perfume, just pain—pain of a stabbed and broken heart that didn't love enough.

I felt if I did love enough, I would love on and on and on, through a hundred million stabbings in my ever-tender heart. I would love as Jesus did, through the tears and through the pain. I would love those stinky sheep with pure love that comes from God.

I didn't want to raise my prickles like an angry, fearful porcupine and stab hurtful people before they could stab me more. I didn't want to retreat into a world of lonely self-protection, licking my festering wounds and wishing to die. Instead, I knew I needed to ask God to heal each wretched stab wound. I needed to choose to love the hurtful people and seek to heal their painful wounds.

I knew I must love them as a mother because they were mine to love, no matter what they did or said, no matter how hurtful they were. I needed to love them as a friend, choosing to love them no matter how hard and how often they stabbed, no matter how ungrateful they were.

Hurtful people are hurting people. They hurt others because they are hurting inside. My dad wrote in a letter, "I compare the wounded saints to a dog who has been injured. It can be the nicest, gentlest animal, but when it is injured it will bite you when you try to help it. We don't beat the injured dog for biting, but seek to hold its mouth while we medicate and bind the wound. To be 'bitten' really hurts, and if you dwell upon it you can really feel bad. But when you understand that you are dealing with someone who is really hurting, you accept it and do what you can to bring healing."

We are healed by the Wounded Healer, so even when we are wounded, we seek to heal others and not to hurt them. We seek to love as we are loved by the One who loved and sacrificed the most. Then our pain gains the fragrance of a healing balm, a perfume to bathe the smelly sheep in beauty. And perhaps they, too, will learn to truly love.

Personal Reflection

Have you been hurt by someone? Is there a person you find hard to love and forgive? Jesus offers His healing for your wounded heart. He knows the pain of being rejected and misunderstood by those close to Him and of being persecuted and scorned by others around Him. Come to Him for healing today.

Write your thoughts here.

Bible Verses

He was despised and rejected by mankind, a man of suffering, and familiar with pain. Like one from whom people hide their faces he was despised, and we held him in low esteem.

Surely he took up our pain and bore our suffering, yet we considered him punished by God, stricken by him, and afflicted.

But he was pierced for our transgressions, he was crushed for our iniquities; the punishment that brought us peace was on him, and by his wounds we are healed. (Isaiah 53:3–5)

Prayer Activities

- Take a few minutes to pray Isaiah 53:3–5 (above) back to God.

- What is God saying to you in response? Write down what you sense He is saying.

HEALING: DAY 3

Insight: Come to Me

JESUS SAYS TO US, "COME TO ME, YOU WHO ARE WEARY AND HEAVY-laden, and I will give you rest. You are so busy for Me, so eager to show that you are following Me, but your soul is weary. Come to Me for rest, for refreshing, for renewal. I see your labor for Me. You work so hard. You sacrifice much. You need My renewing. You need My touch. Let me heal your brokenness and relieve your pain. Let Me restore your soul and pour My life-giving river of renewal and healing into every area of your life. Let Me wash away all that is impure—attitudes and actions that are pulling you away from Me. Humble yourself before Me that I may lift you up.

"Be still before Me. Stop running and doing and accomplishing so many things. I want you, not your service, first of all. Stop pushing and driving yourself and those around you. Take time in My presence daily. Be refreshed and renewed in extended times with Me. Humble yourself and confess your sins before Me. Lead My people into repentance and rest, into quietness and trust in Me. Stop. Stop, my dear one. Stop striving, stop sinning, stop suffering needlessly and causing others to suffer. Stop covering up your pain and brokenness. Confess your sin, your shame, and be healed by the power of My Spirit.

"Come into My presence. Experience My fresh wind, fresh fire. Recommit yourself to Me. Release the pain, the hurt that is weighing you down. Rise up on wings like eagles to see things from My perspective and declare My salvation and truth in My way. Trust in Me alone, not in your own strength, ideas, and programs. Let me lead you gently, quietly, into My way of rest, My path of life. You are troubled and weighed down by so many things. Sit at My feet and discover that this is the best way to learn from Me. Humble yourself before Me. Resist the devil, and he will flee from you. Submit yourself to My Spirit, and I will guide you on paths that are new and refreshing, and I will restore your soul. Trust in Me and be free."

Personal Reflection

Are you weary and heavy-laden today? Do you need refreshing, renewal, and healing? Do you have unconfessed sins weighing you down? God is waiting for you to come to Him and let Him carry your burdens, purify your heart, and heal you.

Write your thoughts here.

Bible Verses

> This is what the Sovereign Lord, the Holy One of Israel, says: "In repentance and rest is your salvation, in quietness and trust is your strength, but you would have none of it …"
> Yet the Lord longs to be gracious to you; therefore he will rise up to show you compassion. For the Lord is a God of justice. Blessed are all who wait for him! (Isaiah 30:15, 18)

Prayer Activities

- Do you need refreshing and renewing today? In what areas of your life do you feel dry and weary?

- What pain, what hurt, is weighing you down? Write a prayer to God, giving Him your pain today.

- Read Isaiah 30:15, 18 (above) out loud. Then sit in quiet with God and let Him refresh you and renew you. Write down any thoughts or pictures He gives you in the quietness.

HEALING: DAY 4

Life Story: Rooted in Heaven

I WAS DESPERATELY HOMESICK. AS I SAT ALONE WITH GOD ON MY HOTEL bed at a ministry retreat, the pain in my heart surged up and streamed down my face. Soggy tissues collected around me.

"I long to be in heaven," I wrote between tear splashes in my journal, "with Jesus's arms around me, where there are no more tears and sorrow and pain, no more struggles and grayness and rain. There we will communicate freely, people will always understand, we will not hurt each other either intentionally or unintentionally … Today I just long—how I long—with an aching, breaking heart, to go to heaven, to go home. I feel so homesick for heaven. I ache and ache inside. My body is racked with weeping. I want to be safe and secure there in Your arms. I want to feel the warmth of Your embrace and hear Your heart beating in love for me. I want to be free to worship You with nothing holding me back. I want to be done struggling, be free from pain, and be full of unclouded joy forever."

I wasn't contemplating suicide. I simply ached for my heavenly home, for the place I would truly belong and be full of joy forever.

In our increasingly unstable world, heaven is our sure eternal home that is waiting for us who are children of God. One day, we will be at home with our Father in heaven. We will see Him face-to-face and rest in His arms. He will wipe the tears of pain and homesickness from our eyes and fill us with everlasting joy in His presence. We need to live in the light of heaven!

A Hungarian friend illustrated for us what it means to have our roots in heaven. He drew a globe with a tree growing from it and said, "This tree has deep roots at this point on earth. It would be difficult to move it to a different place because its roots would have to be yanked up and torn out of the ground."

Then he drew another picture of the world, with a semicircle above it representing heaven. This time, the tree was inverted, with its roots in heaven and its leaves and branches touching the earth. He said, "This tree's roots are in its heavenly home, and the tree provides shelter, fruit, and blessing to many on earth. When God wants this tree to move, He simply rotates the world beneath it, and the tree is easily in another location. There is little pain in the move because the tree's roots are in heaven."

On earth, we face pain, sickness, loss, and death, but God invites us to be rooted in heaven and to ask Him for physical, mental, emotional, relational, and spiritual healing. And one day our pain will be completely healed in heaven.

Personal Reflection

Do you long for heaven, where there will be no more tears or sadness or pain? The joy of heaven can motivate you to keep following Jesus faithfully here on earth, loving God and loving people. And heaven can remind us to pray for healing here on earth, as God invites us to pray for His will to be done on earth as it is in heaven.

Write your thoughts here.

Bible Verses

> For to me, to live is Christ and to die is gain. If I am to go on living in the body, this will mean fruitful labor for me. Yet what shall I choose? I do not know! I am torn between the two: I desire to depart and be with Christ, which is better by far; but it is more necessary for you that I remain in the body.
> Convinced of this, I know that I will remain, and I will continue with all of you for your progress and joy in the faith. (Philippians 1:21–25)

> He will wipe every tear from their eyes. There will be no more death or mourning or crying or pain, for the old order of things has passed away. (Revelation 21:4)

Prayer Activities

- What are you looking forward to in heaven?

- Where are your roots—in heaven or on earth? Write to God about this now.

HEALING: DAY 5

Parable: Flowers of Healing

JESUS AND HIS FRIENDS STROLLED THROUGH A FIELD OF WHITE flowers. They saw a drop of blood on each flower. So many drops of blood, and yet the flowers and the field were more beautiful for them. They wondered how the blood—the evidence of so much pain—could create such beauty. It was like their hearts had been shedding blood droplets of pain through the years, but Jesus collected each one and painted it as a drop of beauty on a white flower. And the flowers were growing strong.

"If it's Your will, please heal our bleeding hearts," they said to Jesus. "Please do what is necessary to heal us completely."

Jesus took His friends to a cliff above a high, narrow waterfall. He invited them to jump down into the pool far below, so they overcame their fear and jumped, falling through the air and sinking deep into the pool.

They saw they were in a cave under the water. Angels came and rubbed healing salve on their wounds, then clothed them in beautiful garments of white rose petals. Jesus healed them and filled them with warmth. Then they shot up from the depths and joyfully danced with Jesus on the water, splashing in the waterfall.

Jesus then raised them high above the waterfall and showed them the dark roofs of their city below. They saw great pain beneath the roofs. Soaring above the city, they sent healing liquid down to the houses. Wherever the healing liquid fell, a vibrant tree sprang up, full of life, breaking through the roofs of opposition and healing the pain. They saw a great tree spring up from within their church—a tree of life, healing, and nourishment. Many people came and were renewed through the tree's fruit. Seeds from the tree were planted in many other churches, and they, too, grew to be healing trees.

Jesus and His friends returned to the field of white flowers, and Jesus's healing power infused even more beauty and life into the flowers. Jesus's friends gathered the flowers and gave them to Jesus. He then accompanied them to give the flowers to those who needed to know He creates beauty from painful, bleeding hearts. Those people, too, received hope for healing.

His shed blood poured into their hearts and healed their wounds. The blood drops were now His healing blood, spreading broadly to bring healing to others.

Personal Reflection

Where do you need healing today? How is Jesus healing your heart? Come to Him with your wounds and hurts. He will heal you and help you bring healing to others. He will comfort you so you can comfort others. He will take your pain and woundedness and create beauty that blesses you and those around you. Trust Him with your pain and woundedness today.

Write your thoughts here.

Bible Verses

> Praise be to the God and Father of our Lord Jesus Christ, the Father of compassion and the God of all comfort, who comforts us in all our troubles, so that we can comfort those in any trouble with the comfort we ourselves receive from God.
> For just as we share abundantly in the sufferings of Christ, so also our comfort abounds through Christ.
> If we are distressed, it is for your comfort and salvation; if we are comforted, it is for your comfort, which produces in you patient endurance of the same sufferings we suffer.
> And our hope for you is firm, because we know that just as you share in our sufferings, so also you share in our comfort. (2 Corinthians 1:3–7)

Prayer Activities

- Where have you experienced physical or emotional healing in your life?

- Ask God who you could comfort with the same comfort you have received. He may bring individual names to mind, or He may give you an idea for a ministry you could join or start. Write what comes to mind and then ask God for help to reach out to them.

HEALING: DAY 6

Prayer and Reflection

JESUS HEALED PEOPLE WITH PHYSICAL SICKNESSES AND DISABILITIES, cast out demons, and offered love and acceptance to the emotionally wounded. His life, death, and resurrection show us that all types of healing—physical, spiritual, mental, and emotional—are found in Him. God invites us to ask Him for healing (but not demand it), believing that He can and does heal people today.

> When Jesus came into Peter's house, he saw Peter's mother-in-law lying in bed with a fever. He touched her hand and the fever left her, and she got up and began to wait on him. When evening came, many who were demon-possessed were brought to him, and he drove out the spirits with a word and healed all the sick. This was to fulfill what was spoken through the prophet Isaiah: "He took up our infirmities and bore our diseases." (Matthew 8:14–17)

Who do you know that needs healing today—physically, spiritually, mentally, or emotionally? Fill in the spaces below for these people and pray for them:

Father God, I bring before You *(name of person needing healing)*:

Please heal them from *(their problem)*:

Thank You that You have the power to heal them. In Jesus's name. Amen.

Father God, I bring before You (name of person needing healing):

Please heal them from (their problem):

Thank You that You have the power to heal them. In Jesus's name. Amen.

Father God, I bring before You (name of person needing healing):

Please heal them from (their problem):

Thank You that You have the power to heal them. In Jesus's name. Amen.

Father God, I bring before You (name of person needing healing):

Please heal them from (their problem):

Thank You that You have the power to heal them. In Jesus's name. Amen.

Look back over the past week on this devotional journey. Write at least one thing you would like to remember from the week.

WEEK 7

Tears of Emotions

My tears have been my food day and night, while people say to me all day long, "Where is your God?" These things I remember as I pour out my soul: how I used to go to the house of God under the protection of the Mighty One with shouts of joy and praise among the festive throng. Why, my soul, are you downcast? Why so disturbed within me? Put your hope in God, for I will yet praise him, my Savior and my God.
—Psalm 42:3-5

As we consider our emotions this week, let's remember God gave emotions to us as a gift. Although we do not let our emotions rule over us, we nevertheless listen to what they are telling us, because through them we can better understand ourselves and grow closer to God and other people.

Lonely Tears

A lonely girl is sobbing quiet tears of pain.
Her friends are gone; will her life ever be the same?
Where is the hope that always twinkled in her eyes,
Now filled with tears from depths of agonizing cries?

She feels despised; no one around her really cares.
She looks for love, not people's apathetic stares.
Will there be one with whom she can share all her fears?
She needs a friend to stand by her throughout the years.

God's love is strong; she knows she can depend on Him.
He goes with her through every trial she is in.
But why the grief? Why is there sadness in her soul?
Why does she cry when she knows God is in control?

Oh, help her, Lord, to see she can depend on You.
You are her friend; Your love will always see her through.
Teach her to love and reach out to those she's around.
She'll find that peace and joy and rest in You abound.

—Annette Carter, age eighteen

Ebenezer Stone: Choose a small, smooth stone and write the word *emotions* on it. Place the stone where you will see it and remember that God knows you and understands your emotions.

EMOTIONS: DAY 1

Parable: Out of the Mud and Mire

JESUS'S FRIEND STOOD WAIST-DEEP IN BARNYARD MUD. SHE FELT MANY emotions as her mind buzzed with so much to be done, and she felt stuck in work that she didn't feel gifted to accomplish.

After reading Psalm 40, she said to Jesus, "Please turn to me and hear my cry. I need You to lift me out of the mud and mire, set my feet on a rock, and give me a firm place to stand. Please give me a new song to sing, a hymn of praise to You, so many will see and fear and put their trust in You. I long to trust You and not anyone or anything else. I need You to work wonders, to show me Your plans. I am poor and needy. Please think of me. You are my help and my deliverer. Oh, my God, do not delay."

As she felt like she was sinking and stinking in the barnyard muck, she remembered that God always made a way for her to stand firm, even in the most discouraging circumstances. He promised to give her His perfect peace and strength for each new day if she focused on Him. He guided her, held her close, and gave her hope. He was her light and salvation. He was the rock that would never move, the foundation that would never be shaken. His love enveloped her and encouraged her, no matter what fears, worries, or frustrations she faced.

She said to Jesus, "I will stand and wait for You. It seems You have not yet heard my cry. You have not yet lifted me from the mud and mire of the barnyard, but someday You will hear my cry and release me from the muck I am stuck in. I will stand in Your strength and wait patiently for You. Someday You will lift me up and set my feet on a rock. Someday You will put a new song in my mouth, a hymn of praise to You. This is where I stand—even in the mud of all the work I don't feel gifted to do—until You move me on, and I will listen to Your voice.

"So I am choosing to accept that I am here in this place for as long as You have me here. I cannot move. I cannot pull myself out of the mud that imprisons my legs and keeps me from soaring or galloping free—or even walking. But I can wait without complaining. I can wait patiently for You to turn to me and hear my cry and give me a firm place to stand and a new song to sing. You make all things beautiful in Your time!"

Personal Reflection

Do you feel stuck in some area of your life today? God invites you to wait patiently for Him. He will turn to you and hear your cry. He will lift you out of the mud and mire and give you a firm place to stand. And when He does, many people will see and fear the Lord and put their trust in Him!

Write your thoughts here.

Bible Verses

> I waited patiently for the Lord; he turned to me and heard my cry. He lifted me out of the slimy pit, out of the mud and mire; he set my feet on a rock and gave me a firm place to stand. He put a new song in my mouth, a hymn of praise to our God. Many will see and fear the Lord and put their trust in him. (Psalm 40:1–3)

Prayer Activities

- In what area(s) of your life do you feel stuck today?

- What emotions are you feeling?

- What do you sense God is saying to you right now? Write what comes to mind.

EMOTIONS: DAY 2

Life Story: We've Read the Last Page

After eight years in Hungary, my husband felt like God might move us toward a different country after our year back in Canada. We left Hungary with the light shining brightly before us, lighting our path for the next year in Regina, Canada, but from that point on, the future was shrouded with darkness. I felt the uncertainty, and I longed to know what lay ahead.

As we waited, I sensed God say to me, "Be patient. Wait. I will give you much more, much better than you ever dreamed."

Those words encouraged me, but when Stephen suggested perhaps God was leading us to a more difficult place to live, I felt afraid. Would God ask us to go to a dangerous place where Christians are persecuted and even martyred?

"Please no, Father. Not me," I said. "It's fine for the Gospel to go forward on the blood of martyrs but not on mine. My blood prefers to be in safer places, more comfortable ones."

In the months that followed, I had a growing sense of foreboding and fear. I wrote in my journal, "I am aching because I'm terrified about going to a closed country and living in constant insecurity and fear. I don't want to go somewhere where people hate us because we're Christian, where we could be imprisoned or tortured or raped or killed, where we live so close to these atrocities that we have to see and even experience them. I just want a home and safety and stability. I don't want to be a hero or a fool and go somewhere that no one wants to go because it is so difficult."

Later that day, I wrote, "I'm so tired of waiting and waiting, Lord. And the worst part is that the direction You seem to be pointing us is one I've never wanted to go in, so I have more of a feeling of impending doom than of anticipation."

A few months later, I read an adventure book to my children. Near the end of the book, nine-year-old Stephanie was so scared that I had to look at the last few pages to prove the story would end well. Seeing the last page helped her endure the frightening circumstances we were experiencing with the characters in the book.

The parallel to our own lives powerfully hit me. We have already seen the last page! If we follow Jesus, we know that no matter what happens, our destination is heaven, where everything is wonderful. That last page of our lives is already written and ready for us to read anytime we feel fearful. Our story will indeed end right. We don't have to fear anything the future holds, no matter where we will be—even in a dangerous place. We've already read the last page!

Personal Reflection

Do you feel afraid about something in the future? Is the path God is pointing you toward one you wish you didn't have to travel? Or is there darkness before you and you don't know what is ahead? God invites you to trust Him and not be afraid. He will hold your hand and guide you each step of the way.

Write your thoughts here.

Bible Verse

> So do not fear, for I am with you; do not be dismayed, for I am your God. I will strengthen you and help you; I will uphold you with my righteous right hand. (Isaiah 41:10)

Prayer Activities

- Write out Isaiah 41:10 as a prayer to God.

    Dear Father, I will not fear,

- What do you sense God is saying to you about your fear?

EMOTIONS: DAY 3

Insight: Preparation for the Future

WHEN GOD GIVES US A SPECIFIC CALLING OR TASK TO PERFORM, He encourages us to be faithful to Him despite our fears or other negative emotions. He says, "My child, do not worry about what you will be doing. I will guide you, lead you, and bless you. Do not be afraid. I am preparing you in these days for great ministry in the days ahead.

"Be faithful in the small things that seem to not fully fit you, so you will be ready when I give you big tasks that would otherwise overwhelm you. These days are not being wasted. You are learning much in preparation for the future. Your work has been significant not only for you but also for the lives that you touched. Do not treat lightly the task I have given you. You are not perfect in it, but you are My chosen one for this task. And I have not called you to be perfect, nor do I expect you to feel perfectly fitted for this job. I am preparing you now for your work and ministry in the future.

"David was not a warrior as he cared for sheep and sang psalms to Me. But that was preparation for him to do what I was calling him toward. Trust Me to guide you and show you what I have planned for you. The highest goal is not your personal fulfillment and satisfaction but My glory.

"Personal satisfaction did not lead Me to die on the cross. Personal satisfaction or even passion for ministry did not lead Me to minister to many hurting people in Israel. Personal satisfaction is a side benefit when you are wholly devoted to Me and release your life, your work, your desires, and your will totally into My hands.

"But in following Me there is always a cross to bear. You are not called to splendor or fame, to comfort and ease, but to sacrifice and suffering, and to great, great blessing. Do not expect great blessing without some suffering, trial, pain, and sorrow.

"Do not keep waiting for your *real* job when you will finally be stress-free and pain-free and everything will be easy. In this world, there will always be struggles, trials, and hardships. Yes, these are hard words, but you must learn to be renewed in your mind and heart and not expect the lie of an easy life or a *perfect* job for you.

"Go in peace and learn to follow Me in my footsteps, in My truth. Walk in My peace and receive My joy. Grow and learn to know and experience My presence and to live and work for My glory to be revealed. Do not fear. Walk in faith. Do not expect a job that will be purely easy. You must grow and learn.

"With growth and change comes discomfort. If you become too comfortable, you become complacent and do not feel your need for Me. Growing and developing means living on the edge, the edge of your comfort zone and the edge of your capabilities. It means pushing yourself out of your comfortable box and stepping into unknown and uncharted territory. Grow and learn, My child."

Personal Reflection

Do you feel stressed about life and about God? Is your heart troubled? Jesus invites you to bring all your emotions to Him and to trust Him as the only way to God.

Write your thoughts here.

Bible Verses

> Do not let your hearts be troubled. You believe in God; believe also in me ... Jesus answered, "I am the way and the truth and the life. No one comes to the Father except through me." (John 14:1, 6)

Prayer Activities

- Reread the paragraphs above and underline the words or phrases that you sense God is highlighting for you today. Write them here.

- Ask God what He would like to say to you today in addition to what you have underlined. Write what you sense He is saying.

EMOTIONS: DAY 4

Life Story: The Gift at the Foot of the Cross

In October of our year in Regina, Canada, I attended a meeting where the speaker shared a vision of the cross. After his moving message, he invited everyone to surrender to Christ at the foot of the large wooden cross in the front of the auditorium. As we sang about Jesus's cross that invites us to surrender our lives to Him and find true life, I felt God urging me to go forward and kneel at the foot of the cross. He invited me to surrender myself to serve Him wherever He would send us, even where Christians are persecuted.

I wept as I knelt and surrendered everything to God—myself, my husband, my children, my pride, my selfishness, and my love of comfort and control—everything I could think of.

As I knelt there, I told God I felt so empty after giving Him all I had. I asked Him for a blessing to fill my emptiness. Then I heard these words, "My presence will go with you and I will give you rest" (Exodus 33:14). I had hoped for something more dramatic, but instead God gave me what I really needed—the promise of His presence and peace.

The next morning, my seven-year-old son "randomly" brought his Bible to me and said, "Look at this funny verse, Mom!" He showed me Exodus 33:14, "My presence will go with you and I will give you rest." He pictured the gifts of God (presents) also going with us and thought the wordplay was funny.

I thanked God for His *presents* on my journey, like the unexpected confirmation of His blessing to me through my seven-year-old son!

Personal Reflection

What do you need to surrender to God today? Are you willing to give every part of your life to Him? Jesus gave up everything—even His own life—for you. He conquered sin and death and rose again, so He is alive, taking care of you today. Are you ready to surrender completely to Him? If you do, you will experience deep and lasting peace.

Write your thoughts here.

Bible Verses

> Moses said to the Lord, "You have been telling me, 'Lead these people,' but you have not let me know whom you will send with me. You have said, 'I know you by name and you have found favor with me.' If you are pleased with me, teach me your ways so I may know you and continue to find favor with you. Remember that this nation is your people."
> The Lord replied, "My Presence will go with you, and I will give you rest." (Exodus 33:12–14)

> Then Jesus said to his disciples, "Whoever wants to be my disciple must deny themselves and take up their cross and follow me. For whoever wants to save their life will lose it, but whoever loses their life for me will find it. What good will it be for someone to gain the whole world, yet forfeit their soul? Or what can anyone give in exchange for their soul?" (Matthew 16:24–26)

Prayer Activities

- Choose a color other than black and doodle about *surrender*. Set a timer for sixty seconds if that helps. Draw or write whatever comes to mind.

- If you are ready, kneel down and surrender yourself completely to God. He will take you just as you are and will give you His presence and His rest.

- Write a prayer to God, telling Him what you are feeling.

- What do you sense God is saying to you? Write it here.

EMOTIONS: DAY 5

Parable: A Tree in the Path

Jesus said to His friend, "Come meet me in the garden." She entered and saw many roses and beautiful, multicolored birds. All over the garden, she saw trees—large, rich, and leafy, with wide trunks and much fruit. And she saw small animals—foxes and others—also around the trees. But it was too crowded—too much busyness in her quiet place.

And she saw a huge tree growing in her path, blocking her way to the gazebo where she would spend time with Jesus. She couldn't reach their place to talk with Him.

Then Jesus cut a doorway and a tunnel through the tree trunk. She walked in and looked up in the darkness. She saw things that could be interesting to explore inside the tree, but Jesus invited her to keep walking and join Him at the gazebo, so she continued out of the tree and followed the path toward Him.

Jesus sat in the light and beauty of the garden gazebo at a small table set for tea. She approached Him, but she couldn't eat or drink because she felt too anxious, so she asked if they could just sit together. They sat on a bench, and she put her head on His chest, but she couldn't speak and couldn't hear His voice. She could only think of the many things she needed to get done and how busy she was. She told Him she needed Him to remove those big trees from her garden. She felt she needed to learn to live in peace all day long, not just when spending concentrated time with Him, and perhaps some of the busyness needed to be removed from her life. She felt unsettled and stressed.

Then a powerful wind blew through the garden like a tornado. She couldn't see anything except whirling leaves, sticks, flowers, tree branches, and even small trees. But in the gazebo with Jesus, there was no wind or confusion. All was calm, clear, bright, and peaceful in that safe space.

After the windstorm, the landscape had changed. The garden was clear of debris and different in its configuration. Then Jesus uprooted the massive tree from her path and transplanted it near a stream outside her garden. She began to relax and rest as her garden became more peaceful and uncluttered.

Personal Reflection

Do you feel pressured and busy, overwhelmed by the many details swirling around you? Do you feel ill-prepared for the day? Do you wonder if it's even possible to be at peace in your busy, nonstop life? Jesus invites you to believe that He is the God of the impossible. He helps you in your weakness and unbelief. He is able!

Write your thoughts here.

Bible Verses

> He has made everything beautiful in its time. (Ecclesiastes 3:11a)

> "Abba, Father," he said, "everything is possible for you." (Mark 14:36a)

Prayer Activities

- Sketch a picture of a garden below, drawing and labeling trees and flowers for each thing that you spend time on, for each part of your schedule.

- Ask Jesus to show you things in your schedule that you need to get rid of and how to do so. Draw a picture of what your life's garden could be, with God's help.

- Go for a walk with Jesus and sit with Him in a quiet place. Ask Him for His peace to permeate your life all the time, every day and night.

EMOTIONS: DAY 6

Prayer and Reflection

G OD GIVES US EMOTIONS TO EXPRESS OUR HEARTS TO HIM, TO others, and to ourselves.

What emotions are you feeling today? Circle the emojis that most closely represent your feelings today.

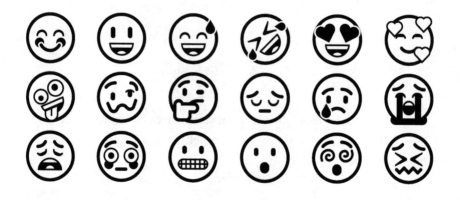

Write a prayer to God telling Him how you feel today.

Galatians 5:22 says, "*The fruit of the Spirit is love, joy, peace, patience, kindness, goodness, faithfulness, gentleness and self-control.*"

Which fruits of the Spirit do you need God to develop in you today?

Ask God to fill you with the fruit you need most.

Write what you sense God is saying to you now.

Look back over the past week on this devotional journey. Write at least one thing you would like to remember from the week.

WEEK 8

Tears of Purpose

And we know that in all things God works for the good of those who love him, who have been called according to his purpose.
—Romans 8:28

He has saved us and called us to a holy life—not because of anything we have done but because of his own purpose and grace.
—2 Timothy 1:9a

God has plans and purposes for each of us to fulfill, but at times we do not see what they are. We can find this confusing or disheartening. This week, we look at how God leads us to follow His plans for us, whether we understand them or not.

I Will Follow in the Dark

I gather all my dreams, my Lord,
and lay them at Your feet.
I raise my head and arms to You
and trust that You will meet
my needs, my inner longings, and
You'll comfort my despair.
I choose to trust in You alone,
believing that You're there.

I do not see the purpose of
Your leading in my past.
I do not know why You have led
and asked me what You've asked.
I do not see the reason for
so much that I have done.
I do not see the way ahead
or how the race is won.

But this I know, that You are good
and strong and wise and true,
so I will follow in the dark,
and I will trust in You.
You are the God who sees my life,
my past and what's to come;
You are the one who holds me fast
and guides what I'll become.
I'll trust in You no matter what
Your path will hold for me.
I'll live my life for You alone.
I'll trust You and be free.

Ebenezer Stone: Choose a small, smooth stone and write the word *purpose* on it. Place the stone where you will see it and remember God's purpose for your life is perfect.

PURPOSE: DAY 1

Parable: Shadow Meets the Great Horse (Part 1)

A SLENDER GRAY MARE NAMED SHADOW TROTTED TOWARD A LARGE group of horses on a wide beach. The horses were all different sizes and colors—tall and short, fat and thin, old and young, black, white, brown, and gray. Shadow gathered with the others around the Great Horse to listen to Him teach about love, sacrifice, and peace.

After teaching them, the Great Horse sent His followers to share His message of hope and love with others. Some plunged into the sea to swim to faraway islands with the message. Others galloped north or south along the beach.

Shadow noticed a powerful golden-brown horse cantering north along the seashore. His mane flowed in the wind as he kicked up little sandstorms and left hoofprints in the sand. He seemed to run in freedom and hope, not in fear. She longed for his joy.

Shadow limped slowly as the horses galloped away. She had been hurt by other horses, so she could no longer gallop freely. As she painfully hobbled northward along the beach, she wondered if she would ever be able to do anything for the Great Horse. He had sent her this way today, but she felt so lame, so wounded, and so, so alone.

Shadow identified with her name—always overshadowed by stronger horses who could do things faster and better than she could. She felt gray and purposeless—like a shadow that flitted and rested aimlessly on the ground. "Why am I even here?" she said with her head hung low. "What can I do for the Great Horse? I'm useless."

The sun beat down on her as it rose higher in the sky. She wondered if she should just turn away and enter the dark forest. Why should she continue in the heat of the wretched sunshine?

But the forest was evil, with vicious wolves, poisonous snakes, and thorny plants, and the Great Horse had sent her this way on the beach. So she decided to continue even though she felt slow and sad and the other horses had long since galloped away to their great tasks. *(To be continued.)*

Personal Reflection

Are you, or is someone you know, wounded and gray, like Shadow? Do you wonder how God could use you to accomplish His purpose? God is inviting you to keep following His way for you even when you feel you have nothing to give.

Write your thoughts here.

Bible Verses

> In your relationships with one another, have the same mindset as Christ Jesus: Who, being in very nature God, did not consider equality with God something to be used to his own advantage; rather, he made himself nothing by taking the very nature of a servant, being made in human likeness.
>
> And being found in appearance as a man, he humbled himself by becoming obedient to death—even death on a cross!
>
> Therefore God exalted him to the highest place and gave him the name that is above every name, that at the name of Jesus every knee should bow, in heaven and on earth and under the earth, and every tongue acknowledge that Jesus Christ is Lord, to the glory of God the Father. (Philippians 2:5–11)
>
> For it is God who works in you to will and to act in order to fulfill his good purpose. (Philippians 2:13)

Prayer Activities

- When Jesus came to earth, He fulfilled God's purposes for Him in every way. Write Philippians 2:5–11 (above) as a prayer to Jesus.

  Jesus, in my relationships with others, please help me have the same mindset as You, who being in very nature God, did not …

- What is God pointing out to you from these verses about your own purpose?

PURPOSE: DAY 2

Parable: Shadow Meets the Great Horse (Part 2)

Shadow limped with her head so low that she saw nothing but the sandy beach beneath her weary hooves. She stopped suddenly as she noticed something soft and golden near her right front hoof. The large golden horse whom she had seen running so joyfully up the beach lay motionless on the sand. His eyes were slightly open, and his face was contorted in pain.

"Hi. My name is Shadow," she said softly. "What happened?"

"My name is Golden," he replied with a strained voice. "I was galloping along the beach, and a shot rang out from the evil forest. It hit my shoulder, and I fell. I can't go any farther." Sweat glistened all over his skin, and his mouth looked dry.

Shadow didn't have the strength to hobble for help, so she stood next to Golden with her shadow covering him. The sun mercilessly beat down on her, but she provided shade for Golden to protect him from the heat.

After some time, the Great Horse galloped up the beach toward them. He stopped and greeted them, then breathed healing onto Golden's shoulder and helped him to stand. The bullet dropped to the ground. Golden was fully healed!

Then the Great Horse turned to Shadow and said, "Your shadow kept Golden alive until I arrived to heal him. Thank you for doing what I sent you to do."

"You sent me this way to be a shadow for Golden?" she asked, with a small shake of her head.

"Yes," the Great Horse replied. "Because you were wounded, you followed him and found him. Because your body was weak and your heart kind, you stayed with him and shielded him from the burning sun. Well done! You are good and faithful. But now I would like to empower you for other service."

Then the Great Horse breathed healing onto her lame leg and into her wounded heart. She felt his power surge through her body and soul. Instead of pain and sadness, she felt wholeness and peace.

"Run powerfully now with Golden, my dear Shadow," said the Great Horse. "And your name will no longer be Shadow. It will be Diamond, because when you were weak and wounded, you were faithful to me. You are as beautiful as a precious diamond."

Golden and Diamond galloped off together, full of healing and strength. Together, they shared their story of healing with many others, who also met the Great Horse and were healed.

As Diamond galloped along the seashore with Golden, she saw the reflection of two horses in the water. One was a powerful, tall golden horse and the other a smaller but equally powerful horse whose hide and mane were no longer a dull gray but instead shone brighter than silver, sparkling like diamonds.

Personal Reflection

Are you willing to bring your pain, weakness, and woundedness to Jesus? Follow Him and be faithful in the things He calls you to do. Even before He heals you, He has purposes and plans for you to fulfill. Be faithful to Him, and He will use you in powerful ways, even in your weakness. And one day, He will heal you and make you strong, to accomplish His purposes in you and through you, for His glory.

Write your thoughts here.

Bible Verses

But he said to me, "My grace is sufficient for you, for my power is made perfect in weakness …"
That is why, for Christ's sake, I delight in weaknesses, in insults, in hardships, in persecutions, in difficulties. For when I am weak, then I am strong. (2 Corinthians 12:9–10)

The nations will see your vindication, and all kings your glory; you will be called by a new name that the mouth of the Lord will bestow. You will be a crown of splendor in the Lord's hand, a royal diadem in the hand of your God. (Isaiah 62:2–3)

Prayer Activities

- Take a few minutes to praise God for using you just the way you are and for giving you strength to do what He has called you to do.

- Ask God what purpose He has for you. Is there a new name He wants to call you (Isaiah 62:2)? Write what He is saying to you.

PURPOSE: DAY 3

Insight: What's the Point?

TIME IS STRANGE. IT MARCHES ON, RELENTLESSLY TICKING, TICKING, ticking toward the future. It doesn't slow down to extend our happier times and doesn't speed up to spare us the pain of hard times. It marches forward, never retreating.

When we live day to day, life can seem to pass quite slowly, but when we think of our lives in light of eternity—past, present, and future—our lives are but a miniscule blip. Blip, blip, blip, each of us is here and then isn't. So what's the point?

We know our purpose in life is to glorify God, to know Him, to become like Him, and to lead others to do the same, but sometimes life seems like just a breath that is here and gone in an instant. Billions of people were born, grew up, and died over the centuries. Billions of little cycles of life are here for a few years and then gone. So what is the meaning? Why are there so many people?

Perhaps each person's life, whether obscure or well-known, whether a day or two long or hundreds of years long, is part of a great tapestry. Or perhaps each face of those who have already lived and those who are yet to live is a tiny picture that is part of the big picture of life and humanity—like the pictures created from thousands of tiny photos combined in a special pattern and order.

If we think of ourselves as just one of billions who live on earth for a short time and then leave, we can feel incredibly small and insignificant. But if we see ourselves and each one around us and all over the world, including those who have died and those who are yet to live, as tiny but unique sections of a beautiful photo picture or a necessary thread in an exquisite tapestry God is creating to display His glory, then we see the meaning of our lives and the lives of all people, both well-known and obscure, who have ever lived and ever will.

We are each a thread in a giant tapestry, an irreplaceable piece of a grand and intricate puzzle, a drop in a bottle of costly perfume, bought at a high price by our Father. This makes it ludicrous for us to be vying for popularity and trying to be number one. It would be like one thread or one droplet of perfume saying to the other, "I'm more important than you are."

At times, we struggle because we want to be somebody and leave an indelible, positive mark on history. We don't want to be just another common leaf that buds, lives, falls, shrivels, and disintegrates, or another nameless face in the vast ocean of faces that make up eternity. But with God, each of us is somebody, and if we follow Him, we fulfill His unique purposes for us. He invites us to live contentedly and joyfully in the perpetual novelty of Himself and what He has planned for us. No moment is ever repeated, and each one counts somehow, in some way, in the big picture. With God's strength, He helps us live each day to the fullest and be content.

Personal Reflection

Have you ever felt overwhelmed by your smallness and insignificance in light of eternity? Do you wonder what your purpose is? Thank God for loving you and making you unique, for His purpose. Thank Him, too, that He has created you to be part of a larger whole, a community where you can find connection and purpose with others.

Write your thoughts here.

Bible Verses

> "For I know the plans I have for you," declares the Lord, "plans to prosper you and not to harm you, plans to give you hope and a future.
> "Then you will call on me and come and pray to me, and I will listen to you." (Jeremiah 29:11–12)

Prayer Activities

- Go for a walk and find a large leaf to press. Write the words of Jeremiah 29:11–12 on it and put it somewhere prominent. Memorize this verse and remember that God loves you and His plans for you are good.

- What do you sense God is saying to you about His plans and purpose for you? Write it here.

PURPOSE: DAY 4

Life Story: The Front Lines

After watching a movie where the hero fought for his country in a war, I filled my journal with questions and thoughts: "Why? Why are we here? Why am I here on earth? There's so much pain in the world: agony, torture, and destruction, and also so much emptiness: complacency, ego-kingdoms, and frivolity." I said with King Solomon, "Meaningless. Everything is meaningless."

I realized only God and His kingdom have meaning. The only reason to exist is to bring glory and honor to Him and lead others to know Him. When the end of all the meaningless luxury and atrocity is over, when everyone will be forever lifted up or forever condemned, the only important thing is how many are around God's throne worshipping Him. Rank and power, wealth and prestige will count for nothing. "Only one life, 'twill soon be passed, only what's done for Christ will last."

I asked myself why I should serve Him on the front lines where the battle was thickest and the casualties most visible. I realized I must do this, even at personal cost, to invite people to know and follow God. If I stayed back when God called me to go, I would most likely become one of the unnoticed casualties—that may outnumber those on the front lines—who are duped into comfort, complacency, and stagnation. The call for me, too, was to fight "for God and my country," but my country was heaven.

I remembered my mandate was to grab others by the hand and say, "Come meet my Father. He's so wonderful, and He loves you so much! He knows you and has been waiting for you to come to Him and be set free from your darkness and bondage. He wants to adopt you as His own child.

"Come! Come to my loving, heavenly Father, all you who are thirsty and tired, empty and lonely. He will fill you, renew you, and embrace you. Come rest in His love. Come close to our Father, you who have strayed away or stayed away from His embrace.

"Join me in His presence. Join me in worship. Join me in inviting others to intimacy with Him. Join me in the celebration, the party before His throne with all the saints and angels in heaven in one voice shouting, whispering, singing, declaring, 'Holy, holy, holy are You, Lord of all.'"

I felt a sense of peace and purpose as I chose to worship God and trust that He would empower me to follow Him and share His message with others.

Personal Reflection

Are you fulfilling God's purpose for you to follow Him wherever He leads you and to invite others to follow Him? If you do this, you will see His power and glory.

Write your thoughts here.

Bible Verse

> I have raised you up for this very purpose, that I might show you my power and that my name might be proclaimed in all the earth. (Exodus 9:16)

Prayer Activities

- Pray this prayer to God:

  Oh God, my Father, move in us by Your power. Stir us out of complacency and stagnation. Soften our hearts to listen to Your Spirit's voice—directly and through others—and to receive Your words with humility, grace, and godly discernment.

  Embolden us to speak Your truth and follow You with uncompromising obedience, no matter how great the cost.

  May we, Your church, arise in unity and power to proclaim the hope of Jesus Christ to a world so confused, so foundation-less, so wounded, and so defiled.

  Awaken us. Enliven us. Empower us. Envelope us in Your loving arms and draw us close to Your tender heart. Fill us with Your passion and fire and guide us into Your kingdom purposes. We are Yours, Father. We long for more of You. May Your Spirit ignite us to blaze forth for Your glory. In Jesus's name. Amen.

- What do you sense God is saying to you in response? Write it here.

PURPOSE: DAY 5

Insight: Don't Quit!

When God gives us a vision and purpose to plan toward, He gives us strength to pursue that vision, even when the road ahead will be hard and will require sacrifice. Consider these words from God for the vision He has given you: "I have called you to a task that will require great courage and humility—a goal, a prize to run toward. Run with perseverance this race marked out for you. Keep your eyes fixed on Me and do not be distracted. Do not give up until you reach the goal.

"Do not become discouraged and quit when the path is hard or dry and boring, or when others do not see the purpose in what you are pursuing. I have not called you to comfort and ease but to battle and triumph. I will go with you and will strengthen and help you. I will give you rest even in the busyness and stress.

"This is a very long-term goal for many years ahead. It will require endurance, perseverance, tenacity, and humility. Put your hand to the plow and do not let it go no matter what winds of coaxing or adversity would seek to persuade you to let go and pursue other 'worthwhile' tasks that are not for you. You will be tempted with good, 'worthy' things, to forsake this calling for 'better,' 'more noble' pursuits.

"You will be tempted by adversities to let go of the plow. Satan will try to peel your fingers back to make you let go, but you must not. You must not! No matter what comes, good or bad, you must not turn aside from the calling I have given you. Do not turn back to easier ways of life.

"Set your face like a flint. Go forth straight as an arrow. Do not turn aside. Do not give way to pressure from without or within. Follow My voice and My leading. Walk in My strength and power every day. Keep the goal in mind at all times. The cost will never be more than you can bear, and you and your family will be richly blessed beyond what you can believe.

"Enter this not as a sprinter for a short stint but as a marathon runner with the far-off goal so clear in your mind that you keep running against all odds. I will go with you and strengthen you. I will show My power in you and through you.

"Oh, My child. Do not give up! Do not quit! Run this race to the end! I will run with you by your side. I will give you strength, courage, and wisdom. I will pick you up when you fall down. Trust in Me and My guidance of you. Trust that My ways and My plans are good.

"Run now. Run to win. Go now, called one, anointed one. Go and do not stop or turn aside. Rise up and run! Heed Me, and you will live abundantly!"

Personal Reflection

What has God called you to do? (If you're not sure, ask Him!) Are you persevering in that calling? God is able to strengthen you and help you not to quit, even when the path is long and wearisome and you wonder what His purposes are in what you are facing.

Write your thoughts here.

Bible Verses

> I press on toward the goal to win the prize for which God has called me heavenward in Christ Jesus. (Philippians 3:14)

> Let us run with perseverance the race marked out for us. (Hebrews 12:1)

Prayer Activities

- What is a long-term calling God has given you? Describe your calling.

- How are you feeling about the race you are running?

- What do you sense God is saying to you right now?

PURPOSE: DAY 6

Prayer and Reflection

GOD INVITES US TO FIND OUR PURPOSE IN HIM.

Respond to God's words in Ephesians 1:3–12 by writing your prayers after each section below:

> Praise be to the God and Father of our Lord Jesus Christ, who has blessed us in the heavenly realms with every spiritual blessing in Christ. (Ephesians 1:3)

I praise You, God, for all the spiritual blessings You give me, like ...

> For he chose us in him before the creation of the world to be holy and blameless in his sight.
> In love he predestined us for adoption to sonship through Jesus Christ, in accordance with his pleasure and will— to the praise of his glorious grace, which he has freely given us in the One he loves.
> In him we have redemption through his blood, the forgiveness of sins, in accordance with the riches of God's grace that he lavished on us. (Ephesians 1:4–8a)

Thank You for choosing me ...

With all wisdom and understanding, he made known to us the mystery of his will according to his good pleasure, which he purposed in Christ, to be put into effect when the times reach their fulfillment—to bring unity to all things in heaven and on earth under Christ.

In him we were also chosen, having been predestined according to the plan of him who works out everything in conformity with the purpose of his will, in order that we, who were the first to put our hope in Christ, might be for the praise of his glory. (Ephesians 1:8b–12)

Father, what is Your will for me? (Write what you sense He is saying.)

Look back over the past week on this devotional journey. Write at least one thing you would like to remember from the week.

WEEK 9

Tears of Suffering

Not only so, but we also glory in our sufferings, because we know that suffering produces perseverance; perseverance, character; and character, hope. And hope does not put us to shame, because God's love has been poured out into our hearts through the Holy Spirit, who has been given to us.
—Romans 5:3–5

Suffering is prolonged pain, extreme discomfort that can seem unbearable. It is being denied something we assumed was a given. Without God, it breeds despair, for there is often no certain ending date. Suffering can leave us with battered, bleeding hearts, yet we can learn to stand firm in humility before God and others, rejoicing! And the blood that bleeds from our breaking hearts mingles with Christ's blood that was shed for us and shouts a testimony of what our mighty God can do with a humble, surrendered life.

My Declaration

I choose to hope when everything seems hopeless.
I choose to wait when stress would bid me flee.
I choose to trust when I am falling, ropeless.
I will affirm Your perfect sovereignty.

I choose Your love when fear would choke and drown me.
I choose Your joy when tempted to despair.
I choose Your peace when storm clouds rage around me.
I will not doubt that You are always there.

I choose Your path, though others would deter me.
I choose Your strength, for all of me is weak.
I choose Your life, though pain and trouble spur me.
I will arise, for You are all I seek.

I seek Your face, not earthly fame or treasures.
I seek Your mind, not foolishness or lies.
I seek Your will, not pandering to others'.
I join Your church in running for Your prize.

I now declare that You are God forever.
I now declare Your love for me is true.
I now declare that You are good forever.
I now submit my life afresh to You.

Ebenezer Stone: Choose a small, smooth stone and write the word *suffering* on it. Place the stone where you will see it, and remember God comforts us in our suffering.

SUFFERING: DAY 1

Parable: Shining Jewels

IN CAVES OPENING ONTO A DARK TUNNEL, JEWELS SHONE BRIGHTLY, illuminating the darkness with their internal flames. A brighter light also shone there—much greater than the collective shining of the many jewels.

Dark water began flowing into the caves. This murky, evil water sought to extinguish the light of the jewels. Some jewels were swept away, their light almost snuffed out. The evil water hungered to quench the light and devour the jewels. The jewels most easily swept away were the ones near the ground—the ones that had been more complacent and less committed to rise to higher levels in the caves.

Then a dark, evil wind began blowing through the caves, also seeking to extinguish the flames burning in the jewels. It sought full darkness for the cave system. But the jewels united to sustain the fire in one another. On their own, they could be snuffed out more easily, but together they were strong.

Then came ravaging wolves—wild, dark, gaunt, powerful, dirty, and ragged, with sharp teeth in snarling mouths. Their goal was to steal, kill, and destroy. They sought to snatch away the jewels and bring them to their evil master.

Then prison bars slammed down in the caves, trapping the jewels but also preventing the wolves from devouring and stealing them. The bars imprisoned the light-bearing jewels and prevented them from freely moving to the passageway or to other caves, but the bars also kept the jewels safe from the wolves.

Despite the prison bars, a great song of praise arose from all the caves—a mighty song of praise to God. The chambers resounded with the praises—the voices of thousands, millions of jewels. The light grew brighter in the powerful songs of praise, and the walls and prison bars started to shake. Then the walls crumbled and fell, the prison bars collapsed, and a great wind of God's Spirit flowed through and fanned the flames even brighter.

A pure, light-filled, life-giving river flowed through the putrid tunnelways and swept away the old structures—the cave walls, floors, and prison bars. When those old structures that contained the darkness were gone, a brilliant sunlight shone everywhere. The river brought life and refreshing, and the sunlight provided light and renewal.

God planted the jewels in fresh, grassy fields, where they grew into flowering, fruitful plants that bore life-giving fruit. The old things had passed away. The days of darkness, terror, attack, and imprisonment were over. Now only life, light, and beauty flourished in grassy slopes, flowers and trees, beautiful green plants, and sunshine. The River of Life brought continued refreshing. The sky was cloudless and blue. All evil was forever gone. The flowers, trees, and plants all raised their voices in praise to their Maker, Sustainer, Deliverer, and Life Giver—the one in whom and through whom and for whom all things were made. Forever and ever.

Personal Reflection

What darkness or trouble are you facing today? Are you willing to praise God even in the hard times and when you feel trapped? As you choose to remain faithful to God and praise Him even in the suffering, He will free and revive you.

Write your thoughts here.

Bible Verses

> About midnight Paul and Silas were praying and singing hymns to God, and the other prisoners were listening to them. Suddenly there was such a violent earthquake that the foundations of the prison were shaken. At once all the prison doors flew open, and everyone's chains came loose. (Acts 16:25–26)

Prayer Activities

- What darkness do you see or feel in your life, family, or community today?

- Write a prayer to God, praising Him for being your Maker, Sustainer, Deliverer, or Life Giver, even in this hard situation.

SUFFERING: DAY 2

Insight: Suffering

When we suffer, either through the lightning bolt of calamity or the stewing pot of everyday life, we have two choices. We can become more tender, or we can become tough and bitter, but we cannot remain unchanged.

Why is suffering necessary? Grapes are crushed or boiled to make grape juice. Lemons and oranges must be cut open with a sharp knife, then forcefully squeezed to extract their juice. Meat is pounded to be tenderized and cooked to be edible.

We peel off the unnecessary husk from a corn cob and put the cob in boiling water to cook. Then we chew the kernels off the cob, savoring their flavor. But when unnecessary husks are peeled from our lives and we are thrown into hot water, we complain. We feel like our lives are being sacrificed. When other people seem to devour all we have to offer, and we feel increasingly bare and spent, we cry out that life is not fair. And we feel, ultimately, that God is not fair.

But suffering is a key to true beauty. Our world says beauty comes from comfort and ease. "You deserve a break today." "You owe it to yourself." We are programmed from birth to fight and avoid suffering. And if the suffering goes beyond our tolerance level, we can become bitter instead of better. We raise our noses and our fists to God instead of humbly bowing before Him and asking Him to soften and teach us through the pain.

Lemons, oranges, and corn are not as tasty unless the unnecessary peeling has been removed. Likewise, we are not as fragrant, tasty, and beautiful unless the outer shell of self-centeredness and pride has been peeled off. But that process hurts. A part of ourselves that we thought we needed is torn away, and we feel naked and vulnerable.

Jesus didn't say, "Avoid stress, struggle, and suffering at all costs." On the contrary, He said, "If anyone would come after me, he must deny himself, and take up his cross daily and follow me. For whoever wants to save his life will lose it, but whoever loses his life for my sake will find it" (Luke 9:23, 24).

Choosing to deny myself means choosing to suffer, because that is what suffering is—being denied something you desire, value, and consider necessary for comfort and happiness. When I choose others' best instead of my own, I deny myself and suffer loss. When I refuse to sin and instead follow God, I choose God's will instead of my own, and I suffer. It's far easier to be a comfort-focused, self-centered, proud, angry person than a Christ-focussed, others-centered, humble, gentle one. However, no comfort can compare with the surpassing greatness of knowing Christ Jesus our Lord. And no suffering is too great if it means I will know Christ better and become more like Him.

Personal Reflection

Are you willing to submit the hard things in your life to God and accept His grace to become more tender instead of tough and bitter? Are there areas of your life where you have chosen the more comfortable path when Jesus is calling you to deny yourself and serve in ways that involve self-sacrifice? God is calling you to follow Him no matter what the cost, and He will reward you with great blessing and joy.

Write your thoughts here.

Bible Verses

> But whatever were gains to me I now consider loss for the sake of Christ. What is more, I consider everything a loss because of the surpassing worth of knowing Christ Jesus my Lord, for whose sake I have lost all things. I consider them garbage, that I may gain Christ. (Philippians 3:7–8)

Prayer Activities

- Write something hard in your life that you can't change.

- Confess any bitterness you have been feeling and offer this hard situation to God. Ask for His grace to help you become more tender instead of tough and bitter.

- Write something you feel God is calling you to do that involves self-sacrifice, but you haven't been willing to do it.

- Confess your unwillingness to follow Him and choose today to say yes to Him, whatever the cost.

- Buy a lemon or orange and squeeze it to make lemonade or orange juice. As you do so, talk to God about following Him even when it is hard. As you drink the juice, listen to His voice. Write what you sense He is saying to you.

SUFFERING: DAY 3

Life Story: Far More, Far Better

When God was directing us toward Central Asia, I wondered at times why I lacked a desire to go there. I wrote to God, "Going to an unknown place in Central Asia doesn't excite me at all. Am I of such little faith? Why do I hope that You will open up something else for us? Is this just like Jesus going to the cross and saying, 'Take this cup from me, but not My will but Yours be done?' Am I just being a Jonah? If You do want us there, will You ever give me a desire and joy to be going there?"

Soon afterward, God gave me a picture that made my stomach tighten and my heart beat faster because of the evil it portrayed. I saw a thin, dark, oval-shaped, almost rubberlike cloud floating toward Central Asia. It stopped over the area, then spread to cover all of the region. It was powerfully evil, and its name was "The Shadow of Death." I shuddered and did not understand what it meant until several weeks later when I read Matthew 4:16, "The people living in darkness have seen a great light; on those living in the land of the shadow of death a light has dawned." What a tremendous promise for all of Central Asia—that they, who lived under the darkness of the Shadow of Death, would see God's great light. My heart filled with joy as I realized God was blessing me with the privilege of going to Central Asia to take part in this unveiling.

I sensed God saying that along with joy, we would also face trials there. He reminded me to be strong in Him and in His mighty power. I sensed He said,

> "Do not fear hard times, but do not be surprised either. I am with you and will help you. I will bear the burdens for you. As you pass through deep waters, I will be with you to carry you. The valley of the shadow of death will not be as dark because My presence and My light will be with you. Do not be afraid. I am with you to strengthen

you and help you, to uphold you with My righteous right hand. Trust Me in all these things, and you will live in peace, no matter what storms rage around you. Trust Me, and you will live."

After we moved to Kazakhstan, we started to experience the great joy that comes with obedience. And as is often the case, most of my fears were unfounded, and we lived in relative peace and security.

Because of God's blessings, I learned to declare wholeheartedly, "Following God is not always easy, but it is always good. God's way is not always the most comfortable, but it is the path of richest, deepest blessing and joy." It wasn't always easy to follow God in Kazakhstan, and life was sometimes hard, but He promised His presence and help each step of the way, and we experienced His blessings that were far more, far better than I could have imagined.

Personal Reflection

What is hard in your life or in the life of a friend or loved one today? Are you surprised by the trials? God has promised that He will be with you and will give you "much more, much better" than you could ever imagine, if you surrender to Him. Take your trials to God in prayer!

Write your thoughts here.

Bible Verses

Dear friends, do not be surprised at the fiery ordeal that has come on you to test you, as though something strange were happening to you. But rejoice inasmuch as you participate in the sufferings of Christ, so that you may be overjoyed when his glory is revealed. (1 Peter 4:12–13)

When Jesus spoke again to the people, he said, "I am the light of the world. Whoever follows me will never walk in darkness, but will have the light of life." (John 8:12)

Prayer Activities

- What trial are you or is someone you know facing today?

- Write a prayer to God, telling Him you will trust Him in this trial, believing that He will shine light in the darkness and will give you "much more, much better" than you could ever imagine.

SUFFERING: DAY 4

Life Story: Joy Outweighs Pain

As I put my infant Joanna to bed one night, my mind was in war-devastated Afghanistan from *Parvana's Journey*, the book I was reading to my older children. I thought about Joanna as a tiny baby coming into this difficult, at times dreadful world and how some people are increasingly pessimistic about the world and its evils, wondering if we should be bringing more innocent, beautiful babies into this wretched place. I thought about the dangers, sorrows, and evils that Joanna might experience in the future and how she wouldn't experience this pain if she hadn't been born.

But then it hit me. If she were never born, she would never have the amazing joy and privilege of knowing Christ and His all-surpassing greatness, His all-encompassing love, His all-comforting presence, His incomprehensible peace, His incomparable fullness, and His unmatchable grace. She would never know the joy of relationship with Him, hearing His voice and communing with Him. She would never know the joy of being His instrument of healing and hope in the lives of others. She would never see His miracles, know His power, or experience His blessing. If she had never been born, she would never be able to call God "Abba Father" and feel secure in the warmth of His deep love.

What a tragedy! What a loss! The surpassing greatness of knowing Christ far, far outweighs the evils and horrors of this dark world. What a message of hope to those who despair over the increasing evil in the world! I rejoiced in the privilege of having been born, of being alive in this world. I felt grateful to be able to raise children to know Christ and live in His all-powerful light in the midst of the great darkness. And I thanked God for His amazing gift of abundant life.

Personal Reflection

Do you wonder why people are born into this world that has so much trouble? Do you fear the future for babies being born? God invites us to trust Him and to believe that He is our purpose for living and that the joy of knowing Him is worth the tears.

Write your thoughts here.

Bible Verses

> Who among you fears the Lord and obeys the word of his servant? Let the one who walks in the dark, who has no light, trust in the name of the Lord and rely on their God. (Isaiah 50:10)

> I keep asking that the God of our Lord Jesus Christ, the glorious Father, may give you the Spirit of wisdom and revelation, so that you may know him better. I pray that the eyes of your heart may be enlightened in order that you may know the hope to which he has called you, the riches of his glorious inheritance in his holy people, and his incomparably great power for us who believe. That power is the same as the mighty strength he exerted when he raised Christ from the dead and seated him at his right hand in the heavenly realms, far above all rule and authority, power and dominion, and every name that is invoked, not only in the present age but also in the one to come. (Ephesians 1:17–21)

Prayer Activities

- Write the names of three people who are struggling or suffering today.

- Pray Ephesians 1:17–21 three times, inserting one name in the blanks each time.

  > I keep asking that the God of our Lord Jesus Christ, the glorious Father, may give _____ the Spirit of wisdom and revelation, so that _____ may know him better. I pray that the eyes of _____'s heart may be enlightened in order that _____ may know the hope to which he has called (him/her), the riches of his glorious inheritance in his holy people, and his incomparably great power for us who believe. That power is the same as the mighty strength he exerted when he raised Christ from the dead and seated him at his right hand in the heavenly realms, far above all rule and authority, power and dominion, and every name that is invoked, not only in the present age but also in the one to come.

- Ask God what He wants to say to encourage one (or more) of the three people. Write here what you sense God is saying.

- If you sense God would have you give them those words, do so.

SUFFERING: DAY 5

Insight: Reaping in Joy

Psalm 126:5–6 speaks of people weeping as they carry the seed and sow it, then singing songs of joy as they reap the harvest and bring home the sheaves. Why do they weep? Maybe from weariness, discouragement, pain, opposition, or oppression.

Weariness. They work and work and are tired, but they keep going!

Discouragement. They work day after day without seeing any results and weep from feeling down about that, but they keep going!

Pain. Perhaps they have physical pain that they bear, but if there is to be a harvest, they must continue despite the fiery pain that screams out with every step they take, so they keep going!

Opposition. Not only do they have their own weakness to contend with, but perhaps they have opposition against them from the outside. Perhaps their tears are from people scorning them, discouraging them, physically hurting them, or taunting them, but they keep going!

Oppression. Perhaps their tears are from spiritual oppression. As they fight to continue, the battle they wage takes so much out of them, yet they keep going!

Despite the physical, emotional, social, and spiritual struggles of continuing to sow the seed day after day, with no results or harvest to be seen, if they do not give up, they will one day experience and enjoy the great harvest. Their aching hearts and tear-filled eyes will be filled instead with joy, and joyful songs will be on their lips.

When the work is hard and we see no results, when discouragement brings tears to our eyes, the important thing is not to stop weeping but to keep working! Jesus doesn't say the weeping is wrong but rather that, with the weeping, we continue sowing to completion. Then there will be a joyful harvest. Perhaps we will never see the harvest of the work we do here, or we will see only a small portion of it, but we keep going.

Some of us stop working, sit down, and feel sorry for ourselves when we weep. We feel discouraged because we are discouraged, and then there is no joyful harvest whatsoever, because we quit. If we get discouraged and stop because either we see no results or we feel like there never will be results, there surely never will be any results because we have quit! But if in the midst of discouragement and weeping, we keep working, then someday we will experience a joyful harvest.

Personal Reflection

Are you, or is someone you know, tempted to quit? If in the midst of discouragement and weeping, they persevere, someday there will be joyful results. Your encouragement can help give them strength to persevere.

Write your thoughts here.

Bible Verses

> Those who sow with tears will reap with songs of joy. Those who go out weeping, carrying seed to sow, will return with songs of joy, carrying sheaves with them. (Psalm 126:5–6)

> The end of the matter is better than its beginning, and patience is better than pride. (Ecclesiastes 7:8)

> But encourage one another daily, as long as it is called "Today," so that none of you may be hardened by sin's deceitfulness. (Hebrews 3:13)

Prayer Activities

- Look at the descriptions of weariness, discouragement, pain, opposition, or oppression above. Which do you most often experience? Are you facing one or more of these now? Write a prayer asking God to help you persevere even while you are "sowing in tears."

- Who is someone you can encourage today? Do you know someone who seems to be struggling on their journey? Ask God what He would like you to say to encourage them and write it here. Then write a note to them, encouraging them to persevere, even in their suffering.

SUFFERING: DAY 6

Prayer and Reflection

In Psalm 142, David writes his lament to God and tells Him his trouble. He then cries out to God for help. Finally, he ends with hope.

> I cry aloud to the Lord; I lift up my voice to the Lord for mercy. I pour out before him my complaint; before him I tell my trouble.
>
> When my spirit grows faint within me, it is you who watch over my way. In the path where I walk people have hidden a snare for me. Look and see, there is no one at my right hand; no one is concerned for me. I have no refuge; no one cares for my life.
>
> I cry to you, Lord; I say, "You are my refuge, my portion in the land of the living." Listen to my cry, for I am in desperate need; rescue me from those who pursue me, for they are too strong for me. Set me free from my prison, that I may praise your name. Then the righteous will gather about me because of your goodness to me. (Psalm 42:1–7)

Write your own psalm to God now.

> *Lord, I pour out before You my complaint; I tell You my trouble:*

I cry to You, Lord; I say, "You are:

Because of Your goodness to me, this is my hope:

Look back over the past week on this devotional journey. Write at least one thing you would like to remember from the week.

WEEK 10

Tears of Encouragement

Encourage one another and build each other up.
—1 Thessalonians 5:11

But encourage one another daily, as long as it is called "Today,"
so that none of you may be hardened by sin's deceitfulness.
—Hebrews 3:13

When we encourage someone, we infuse them with courage, giving them reason to persevere when life is hard, helping them not be torn down by inner or outer pressures, and building up their strength. As God and others encourage us, we can in turn encourage those around us.

Wanted—Dead or Criticized

Silently they scream—
    Scream as harsh words
        Pierce the core of their tender hearts.

They scream out (though silently)
    Against the subtle, cutting cruelty
        Shown to them by fellow man.

"Can't I say anything?" they ask bitterly,
    "Without someone cutting me down?
        "Can I do nothing right?" is their cry.

My heart aches for them.
    I hurt, too, so much, when they are hurt
        By the thoughtlessness of others.

I cringe, too, in my heart,
    At the sharp words
        Spoken to them with careless flippancy.

O God, I pray that I may help
    Those who are hurting,
        That I might soothe their wounds
            With Your love.

—Annette Carter, age fourteen

Ebenezer Stone: Choose a small, smooth stone and write the word *encouragement* on it. Place the stone where you will see it and remember to encourage others daily.

ENCOURAGEMENT: DAY 1

Parable: A Lake of Roses

Thousands of roses grew close together in a lake of pure, clear water. They covered the lake in a carpet of blossoms, their fragrance filling the air and their stems drawing refreshment from the water. Jesus's friends waded into the water among the roses, inhaling their fragrance and delighting in their beauty. Immersed to their necks in the water, they looked around and saw roses in every direction, filling their senses. They felt their bodies being renewed.

After being refreshed among the roses, they waded toward the shore, collecting many roses in their arms. The roses had no thorns—only beauty, healing, and refreshing. Jesus's friends carried the roses and walked onto the beach.

Then they laid down the roses to form a path that led toward the Lake of Roses. The path was for others to follow so they also could discover the renewing water. They quietly laid down rose after rose as an offering of beauty to God and of love to others who through this path would find the way to deep refreshing, just as Jesus's friends had experienced.

When the path was finished, they heard a great crowd of people approaching. Jesus's friends stepped out of the way so the others could follow the rose path to the Lake of Roses. The path led them to greater depths of life, healing, and beauty in God. When the people rose up from the water, God sent each one out with greater purpose, peace, and joy in Him.

Those people also filled their arms with roses for others. Some used the roses to bring deep healing to those who were unable or unwilling to come to the Lake of Roses. Others used the roses to create beautiful artwork that pointed people to God. Each one took the roses from the lake to accomplish God's purpose in them and through them to others—purposes that brought them great joy and refreshing. And God's Spirit continually replenished the Lake of Roses by His power.

Personal Reflection

Do you need refreshing today? Come to God for encouragement. Turn away from whatever is keeping you from Him and experience His refreshing, His healing, His beauty, and His rest. Then take those "roses" and share them with others in the ways God equips you, so they, too, can be encouraged.

Write your thoughts here.

Bible Verses

> Let us hold unswervingly to the hope we profess, for he who promised is faithful. And let us consider how we may spur one another on toward love and good deeds. (Hebrews 10:23–24)

Prayer Activities

- Ask God to bring four friends to mind who need an encouraging card or text today. Write their names below.

- Ask God to give you an encouraging Bible verse or encouraging words for them and write them next to their names.

- Write a text or card to them, including those encouraging words.

- Pray for them and give it to them!

Friend #1:

Friend #2:

Friend #3:

Friend #4:

ENCOURAGEMENT: DAY 2

Insight: Encouragement from God

Sometimes we are like Jeremiah, Moses, or Gideon, who made excuses when God called them to do something difficult. But He encourages us to boldly follow Him.

Jeremiah said, "Ah, Sovereign Lord, I do not know how to speak; I am only a child" (Jeremiah 1:6).

Moses said, "Who am I that I should go? ... What if they do not believe me or listen to me? ... Pardon your servant, Lord. I have never been eloquent ... I am slow of speech and tongue ... Please send someone else" (Exodus 3:11; 4:1, 10, 13).

Gideon said, "How can I save Israel? My clan is the weakest in Manasseh and I am the least in my family" (Judges 6:15).

God encouraged each of them to trust Him and to let Him do the work He was calling them to do. And He used them powerfully, despite their qualms and hesitations.

At times, we, too, make excuses when God asks us to do something that feels too big and out of our comfort zone. And we, too, need encouragement.

We might say, "I'm not ready, Lord! I'm not good enough for this. I don't have enough experience, God. Don't You understand?" But God encourages us, saying, "My child, I know you. I created you and chose you. I am enough for you. With My help, you are indeed ready. Be courageous and get going!"

Another excuse we might throw at God is "I don't have time, Lord! I'm too busy right now. I'll have more time later." But God encourages us, saying, "Just serve Me now with what I have given you. I've prepared you for what I am asking you to do. Be courageous and get going!"

A third excuse we might have is "I'm too wounded, Lord. You know my past, my failures, my struggles, all that I've been through. You can't use someone as broken and useless as I am." But God encourages us, saying, "If you will allow Me, I will use your flaws to create something beautiful. Be courageous and get going!"

God encourages us to trust Him and do the things He calls us to do without avoiding the hard things or making excuses. God has prepared us and called us, and He is enough!

Personal Reflection

Has God been asking you to do something for Him that you feel is too hard, too big for you, or just plain terrifying? Have you been avoiding it? Don't dismiss the hard things or make excuses. God has prepared you and called you, and He is enough.

Write your thoughts here.

Bible Verse

> Have I not commanded you? Be strong and courageous. Do not be afraid; do not be discouraged, for the Lord your God will be with you wherever you go. (Joshua 1:9)

Prayer Activities

- What is something hard God has given you to do or is calling you toward?

- What excuses do you make or are tempted to make to say you are not adequate for what God is asking you to do?

- Come to God just as you are, with your abilities and inabilities, your strengths and weaknesses, your wholeness and brokenness. Write a prayer asking Him to encourage you and empower you to do the things He is calling you to do.

ENCOURAGEMENT: DAY 3

Life Story: Calgary Storm

After I earned my PhD at the University of Toronto, I experienced a season of disappointment. Toward the end of my degree, God started impressing on our hearts that He wanted us to move to Calgary the following fall. Although we had been working overseas for many years, we sensed God wanted us to settle in Calgary and not move any more. But there were many questions and uncertainties.

In January of my final PhD year, by faith, my husband resigned from his work on June 30, and we started pursuing jobs in Calgary. Nothing permanent opened up, but God led us to be International Workers in Residence for a year at Ambrose University. We moved to Calgary and still didn't know what God had planned for us after that year.

In August, I felt like God said to me, "Wait for Me, My child. I will show you great and wondrous things that you do not know. You feel the pain of loss. You feel the weariness of the past months and years, even decades, of preparation. Joy will come. Wait for Me and do not despair. You are not alone. Wait for me. Take courage. I am with you in the darkness and pain. From the ashes of burnt-up hopes and dreams, I will create beauty and life in amazing ways that will continually surprise you. Rest in Me. Center your soul on Me."

By the following January, it was clear nothing was opening up for us in Calgary. We pursued overseas options as well. Nothing. What was God doing? What would we do after April? I felt my hopes and dreams being consumed by fire.

Walking through a forest one day with my mentor, I picked up a pine cone. My mentor explained that this kind of pine cone only opened with a forest fire. Its potential for growth only came with extreme heat. I pictured a forest fire raging through that area. As the fire consumed all the plants, trees, dead wood, and excessive undergrowth, it also released seeds from the pine cones. New trees grew from the ashes. A new season arrived. As I listened, I wondered what God would create from the ashes of my dreams.

After discouraging months of waiting and wondering what God was planning for us, He opened doors for us in Toronto and provided ministry that we hadn't imagined but that was exactly what He had been preparing us for. Beauty arose from the ashes—new life from the devastation and new hope after the destruction. I felt encouraged.

Personal Reflection

Is someone you know facing a fiery trial that is burning up their dreams, plans, and hope? God invites you to encourage them to seek His perspective on the fire that is raging. He will bring beauty from the ashes and will give them courage.

Write your thoughts here.

Bible Verses

> The Lord has anointed me ... to bestow on them a crown of beauty instead of ashes, the oil of joy instead of mourning, and a garment of praise instead of a spirit of despair. (Isaiah 61:1, 3)

Prayer Activities

- Go for a walk and choose a pine cone or print a photo of a pine cone from the internet to remind you of how God brings beauty from ashes.

- Ask God to bring beauty from the ashes in your life.

- Listen to "Rise" by Ashes Remain. https://www.youtube.com/watch?v=zKdzoiXXh-o

- Who is a broken soul you can pray for or encourage today? Ask God to show you how to let the fire inside you shine brightly to meet their needs. Write what you sense He is saying.

- Ask God to give you a message of encouragement to pass on to a stranger. Maybe it will be a store clerk or a person on a park bench. Write the message here. Then write it on a piece of paper to take with you to give to a "random" person that He will point out to you.

ENCOURAGEMENT: DAY 4

Insight: Consider Jesus

When life is difficult, we can find ourselves lacking hope and losing heart. But as we look toward Jesus, He encourages us to persevere.

Jesus didn't lose heart in the many quiet years in the carpenter's shop. Instead, He grew in wisdom and stature and in favor with God and people.

He didn't lose heart in the desert when hunger overwhelmed Him and the enemy tempted Him in His most vulnerable spots. Instead, He wielded God's Word as a weapon and stood firm.

He didn't lose heart when hundreds of smelly, pushy people mobbed Him to minister to them. Instead, He loved, touched, and healed them.

He didn't lose heart when sinful men opposed Him and falsely accused Him. Instead, He was silent and submitted to God's plan.

He didn't lose heart when even His dearest friends misunderstood and deserted Him. Instead, He looked on them in love.

He didn't lose heart when He was betrayed and put to death by cruel, violent men. Instead, He took our sins upon Himself and rose from the dead so we could be free and have eternal life, and so we could run this race and know our goal is heaven.

Jesus kept His eyes fixed on the joy set before Him, and from this joy, He gained courage and strength to face hardships and death. And then He rose from the dead and is alive in heaven today!

Personal Reflection

Is someone you know losing heart today? Jesus invites us to encourage them to turn their eyes toward Him, keep their focus continually on Him, and draw their strength from Him. He will give them hope and carry them through.

Write your thoughts here.

Bible Verses

> Fixing our eyes on Jesus, the pioneer and perfecter of faith. For the joy set before him he endured the cross, scorning its shame, and sat down at the right hand of the throne of God. Consider him who endured such opposition from sinners, so that you will not grow weary and lose heart. (Hebrews 12:2–3)

Prayer Activities

- Who do you know that is losing heart today? Describe their situation here.

- Write a prayer asking God to encourage them to focus on His power and goodness and not on their stressful circumstances and brokenness.

- Think of three people you know who have faced struggles but persevered. Write their names in the first space of each line below. Then fill in the lines with their struggle and how they persevered.

    1. _____ didn't lose heart when ...

    Instead, they ...

    2. _____ didn't lose heart when ...

    Instead, they ...

    3. _____ didn't lose heart when ...

    Instead, they ...

- Thank God for these people and pray God's blessing on them, asking Him to encourage them and help them to continue to stand strong for Him.

ENCOURAGEMENT: DAY 5

Insight: The Blessing

A POWERFUL FORM OF ENCOURAGEMENT IS TO SPEAK WORDS OF blessing to others. Consider the power and beauty of blessing others as you read these words of blessing for a group of intercessors in Toronto:

> I bless you to be a light for Jesus, to sing His praises and to stand strong for Him even in a culture that denies Him and seeks to cancel you for your belief in His truth. I bless you to raise His praise to the highest heaven and to the ends of the earth, that at the name of Jesus, every knee should bow, in heaven and on earth and under the earth, and every tongue confess that Jesus Christ is Lord, to the glory of God the Father (Philippians 2:10–11).
>
> I bless you to love and cherish our Indigenous brothers and sisters, not to lord it over them in any way but to humbly seek to know them, respect them, and love them as brothers and sisters, mothers and fathers, sons and daughters (Mark 10:29–31, 42–45). I bless you to act justly, love mercy, and walk humbly with our God and with our Indigenous neighbors (Micah 6:8).
>
> I bless you to stand up for Jesus in the public sphere with your words, your votes, and your interest in the politics and politicians of our country. If we are silent, who will speak up for those who cannot speak for themselves, for the rights of all who are destitute? I bless you to speak up and judge fairly, to defend the rights of the poor and needy (Proverbs 31:8–9).
>
> I bless you to rejoice in the Lord always, even in your suffering (Philippians 4:4, Romans 5:3). I bless you to come to Him with your weariness and burdens and find rest for your souls as you take His yoke upon you and learn from

Him, for He is gentle and humble in heart, and His yoke is easy and His burden is light (Matthew 11:28–30).

And finally, I bless you to remain in Jesus as a branch remains in the vine and to bear much fruit. I bless you to keep His commands and to remain in His love, so whatever you ask in His name, He will give you (John 15:5–10). Our God is able to do immeasurably more than all you could ask or imagine, according to His power at work in you, for His glory in the church and in Christ Jesus throughout all generations, for ever and ever. Amen (Ephesians 3:20–21)!

Personal Reflection

Have you thought about the power of your words? Are your words to people and about people negative or positive? Positive words based on God's truth can bless people in powerful ways. We must choose to encourage people by blessing them with our words.

Write your thoughts here.

Bible Verses

The Lord bless you and keep you; the Lord make his face shine on you and be gracious to you; the Lord turn his face toward you and give you peace. (Numbers 6:24–26)

Prayer Activities

- Take time today or tomorrow to encourage someone by speaking to them the blessing above or the following words of blessing based on Numbers 6:24–26:

The Lord bless you
with abundant blessings from the vast storehouse
of His delightful goodness,
and keep you
in the palm of His hand, close to His loving heart, safe
from anything that would pull you away from Him.
The Lord make His face shine upon you
with warmth and favor, even as the spring sunshine brings new life and
vibrancy to the death-bitten landscape all around, and be gracious to
you, in His infinite love and mercy always giving you another chance.
The Lord turn His face toward you,
with compassionate eyes that really see you, patient ears
that always hear you, a gentle tongue to teach and encourage
you, and a loving smile to give you strength to go on,
and give you peace,
the peace that rests secure and unruffled in the midst of even
the wildest, most frightening and tempestuous storms.

- Write your own words of blessing for someone and speak them or send them to the person.

ENCOURAGEMENT: DAY 6

Prayer and Reflection

Look back over all you have read, written, drawn, and heard from God in the past ten weeks on this devotional journey.

What is something you read that encouraged you? How did it encourage you?

Which prayer activity encouraged you most? How did it encourage you?

What is something God said to you that encouraged you? How did it encourage you?

Who can you share at least one of these things with, that they, too, may be encouraged?

Praise God for His love, patience, and guidance. What is He saying to you now? Write it here.

Write your response to God for all He has been doing and is continuing to do in your life.

FAREWELL!

Thank you for journeying with me through the past ten weeks as I shared my heart with you and God's heart for you in *The Gift of Tears*. I hope you have been enriched and encouraged in your own life and have been strengthened to love and serve God and others.

I encourage you to write your own *Gift of Tears* stories and poems to help you remember the ways God has blessed you in your difficult times and to inspire others toward greater closeness with Jesus. Keep journaling your times of talking and listening to Him as a written testimony of God's grace and power.

As you continue your journey, I invite you to pray this prayer with me:

You Are – I Choose

You are my Light in the darkness;
You are my Joy in the pain;
You are my Comfort in sorrow;
You are my Friend in the rain.

You are my Hope when I'm hopeless;
You are my Strength when I'm weak;
You are my Shade in the desert;
You are the Shelter I seek.

You are my Peace when I'm broken;
You are my Guide when I'm lost;
You are my Refuge in trouble;
You hold me close when I'm tossed.

You are my Reason for living;
You are my Wisdom and Love;
You are my Shepherd, Protector;
You are my Father above.

I choose to follow you always;
I choose your way and your will;
I choose to fully surrender;
I choose to rest and be still.

I choose to not be discouraged;
I choose to not demand why;
I choose to thank you for giving
The gift of tears that I cry.

You are my King and my Hero;
You are my Savior and Friend;
You are my Treasure forever;
You bless my life to the end.

May the God of hope fill you with all joy and peace as you trust in him, so that you may overflow with hope by the power of the Holy Spirit. (Romans 15:13)

Now to him who is able to do immeasurably more than all we ask or imagine, according to his power that is at work within us, to him be glory in the church and in Christ Jesus throughout all generations, for ever and ever! Amen. (Ephesians 3:20-21)

NOTES

1. Max Lucado, *You are Special* (Wheaton, IL: Crossway Books, 1997).
2. Henri J. M. Nouwen, *The Return of the Prodigal Son: A Story of Homecoming* (New York, NY: Image Books, 1994), 43.
3. Mark Buchanan, *Spiritual Rhythm: Being with Jesus Every Season of Your Soul* (Grand Rapids, MI: Zondervan, 2010).
4. Judith Viorst, *Alexander and the Terrible, Horrible, No Good, Very Bad Day* (New York, NY: Aladdin Paperbacks, 1987).

CPSIA information can be obtained
at www.ICGtesting.com
Printed in the USA
JSHW080451270623
43834JS00002B/8